Google for the Older Generation

by
Noel Kantaris

Bernard Babani (publishing) Ltd
The Grampians
Shepherds Bush Road
London W6 7NF
England

www.babanibooks.com

Please Note

Although every care has been taken with the production of this book to ensure that all information is correct at the time of writing and that any projects, designs, modifications and/or programs, etc., contained herewith, operate in a correct and safe manner and also that any components specified are normally available in Great Britain, the Publishers and Author(s) do not accept responsibility in any way for the failure (including fault in design) of any project, design, modification or program to work correctly or to cause damage to any equipment that it may be connected to or used in conjunction with, or in respect of any other damage or injury that may be so caused, nor do the Publishers accept responsibility in any way for the failure to obtain specified components.

Notice is also given that if equipment that is still under warranty is modified in any way or used or connected with home-built equipment then that warranty may be void.

© 2012 BERNARD BABANI (publishing) LTD

First Published - August 2012

British Library Cataloguing in Publication Data:

A catalogue record for this book is available from the British Library

ISBN 978 0 85934 738 9

Cover Design by Gregor Arthur

Printed and bound in Great Britain for Bernard Babani (publishing) Ltd

About this Book

You must have heard the expression 'Google it', which is rapidly becoming the standard reply whenever you ask someone a question and they don't know the answer! Google has become the key to our thirst for finding answers, but it is more than just an Internet search tool. *Google for the Older Generation* has been written both to help you use Google Search more effectively, and to explore some of the myriad of tools that come with it. The book includes chapters on:

- Using Google to **Search the Web** more effectively, dealing with special search features, such as weather, global times, air travel, etc.

- Organising your daily life with the **Google Calendar** and your correspondence with **Google Mail**.

- Using **Google News** and **Finance** to easily keep abreast of world and local news as and when it happens and to get instant up-to-date information on financial matters.

- Using **Google Plus** to share photos and videos with friends and family.

- Exploring **Google Drive**, used to store your important documents, spreadsheets, presentations or drawings and be able to access them from wherever you happen to be in the world.

- Creating a **YouTube** account, watching videos, and uploading your own videos to **YouTube**.

- Using **Google Maps** to view maps and get information on local services, public transport, driving and traffic conditions, view satellite and 'walk through' **Street View** imagery of many parts of the world.

- Use **iGougle** to produce your own personalised Google page by arranging for news, photos, weather and anything else you choose to be in front of you when you open your Internet browser.

- 'Flying' with **Google Earth** to anywhere on the globe to view satellite imagery, aerial and **Street View** photography.

This book is produced in full colour and is presented using everyday language and avoiding technical jargon wherever possible. It was written with the Older Generation in mind who may have little knowledge of using a computer. It will, of course, also apply to all other age groups. Google frequently makes changes to its programs, so if something I show is not quite the same, that is probably why. Have fun and enjoy Googling!

Please note that some parts of this book are based on my previous book 'An Introduction to Google for the Older Generation' that I co-authored with Phil Oliver. However, any material used has been completely revised and updated to cover the enormous number of changes and additions that have been made by Google.

About the Author

Graduated in Electrical Engineering at Bristol University and after spending three years in the Electronics Industry in London, took up a Tutorship in Physics at the University of Queensland. Research interests in Ionospheric Physics, led to the degrees of M.E. in Electronics and Ph.D. in Physics. On return to the UK, he took up a Post-Doctoral Research Fellowship in Radio Physics at the University of Leicester, and then a lecturing position in Engineering at the Camborne School of Mines, Cornwall, (part of Exeter University), where he was also the CSM Computing Manager. Lately he also served as IT Director of FFC Ltd.

Books by the Same Author

BP738	Google for the Older Generation
BP284	Programming in QuickBASIC
BP259	A Concise Introduction to UNIX
BP258	Learning to Program in C
BP250	Programming in Fortran 77

Books Written with Phil Oliver

BP726	Microsoft Excel 2010 Explained
BP719	Microsoft Office 2010 Explained
BP718	Windows 7 Explained
BP710	An Introduction to Windows Live Essentials
BP706	An Introduction to Windows 7
BP703	An Introduction to Windows Vista
BP590	Microsoft Access 2007 explained
BP585	Microsoft Excel 2007 explained
BP584	Microsoft Word 2007 explained
BP583	Microsoft Office 2007 explained
BP581	Windows Vista explained
BP580	Windows Vista for Beginners
BP557	How Did I Do That ... in Windows XP
BP550	Advanced Guide to Windows XP
BP538	Windows XP for Beginners
BP525	Controlling Windows XP the easy way
BP514	Windows XP explained
BP498	Using Visual Basic

Acknowledgements

Thanks to friends and colleagues for their helpful tips and suggestions which assisted in the writing of this book.

Trademarks

Android, **Chrome**, **Google**, **Gmail**, **iGoogle** and **YouTube** are registered trademarks of Google Inc.

All other brand and product names used in the book are recognised as trademarks, or registered trademarks, of their respective companies.

Contents

1

Google – the Search Engine

Google is practically everybody's favourite Internet search engine, which we have been using since the late 1990s. It is a tool for finding information and resources on the World Wide Web. If you use the Internet, at some time or other you'll most probably need to use a simple Google search to find what you are looking for.

Google, however, is much more than just a simple search tool. It organises the world's knowledge and keeps indexes of Web pages and other online content such as photos, movies, books, news, maps, scholarly papers, videos, music and information on several different type of services, and makes these freely available to anyone with an Internet connection. To pay for all this, Google generates its income with unobtrusive online advertising and places them on one side of its search results pages.

Google Query Processor

A Google search query normally lasts less than a second, yet involves a number of different steps that must be completed before you get the search results on your screen, as shown in Fig. 1.1. The Query Processor includes the **Search** box, the 'Engine' that evaluates and matches the query to the most relevant documents, and the 'Results formatter' that presents the results of the query on your screen. The process involves the following steps:

- You type a query in the **Search** box. The query is checked for sentence structure and if it is not spelled correctly, a more popular or correct spelling variation is displayed for your consideration.

- The query is then sent to Google's Web Server to check if it is relevant to their search databases (such as News, Books, Images, Maps, Earth, Videos, etc.), and relevant links are attached to the regular search query and sent to the Index Servers.

- In the Index Servers a list of relevant pages for the query is prepared and ranked on page content, usage and link data, and a list of relevant adverts is chosen for placement near the search results.

- The query then goes to Google's Doc Servers, which retrieve the stored documents and generate short 'snippets' describing each search result which are then returned to you – all in a fraction of a second.

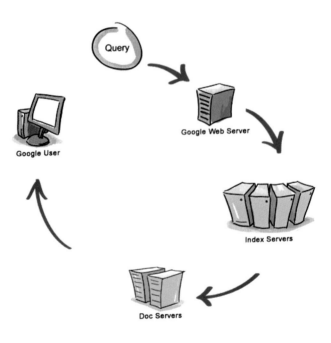

Fig. 1.1 The Life of a Google Search Query.

Searching the Web

Using Google to carry out a Web search is easy, but with a little more knowledge, you can get much more out of it. For a basic search in the UK, type **www.google.co.uk** into your browser's **Address** bar (we use the Internet Explorer as our browser), which displays the screen shown in Fig. 1.2 below.

Fig. 1.2 Google Search Home Page for the UK.

Then type your query (one word, or a phrase) that best describes the information you are interested in into the **Search** box and either, accept a drop-down **Instant Search** option, press the **Enter** key, or click the **Search** button (see Fig. 1.3). Most Web browsers also have a **Search** box that lets you search the Web directly from the **Address** bar.

Google produces a results page, similar to the one shown in Fig. 1.4, with a list of Web pages related to your search terms. It ranks the list with what it considers the most relevant match found at the top. Clicking any underlined link in the results list will take you to the related Web page.

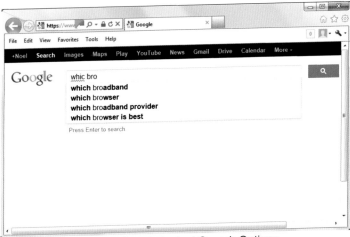

Fig. 1.3 A Google Instant Search Options.

Note that in our example, Google recognised our typo, and searched for **which browser**, not **whic browser**.

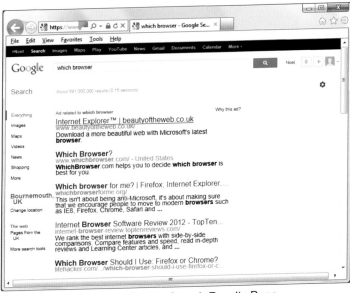

Fig. 1.4 A Google Search Results Page.

The Search Results Page

The results page contains lots of information about the search. Here we show and describe the parts of the page, starting from the top, and working from left to right.

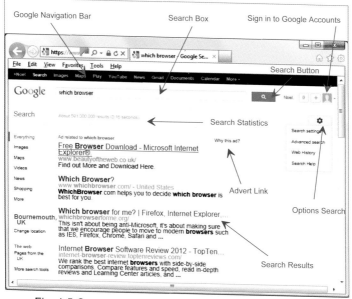

Fig. 1.5 Components of a Google Search Results Page.

Google Navigation Bar – Click the link for the Google service you want to use. You can search the Web, browse for images, videos, maps, news, shopping, navigate to **Gmail** or click on the More link to access other Google tools.

Search Box – The text box where you type your search terms to start a Google search.

Search Button – Click this button to send a search query. This is the same as pressing the **Enter** key.

Page Title – The first line of any search result item is the title of the Web page found and sometimes the URL (Uniform Resource Locator) of the site. The text beneath the Page Title is an excerpt from the results page with the query terms emboldened.

Search Statistics – This describes your search, indicating the total number of results, and how long the search took to complete (0.16 seconds in our example).

Search Options – These let you select search settings, such as safe search filters, use exact search words or phrases, manage your Web history so you can get the most relevant to your results, or get search help. Below we show in Fig. 1.6 the screen for the **Advanced search** option.

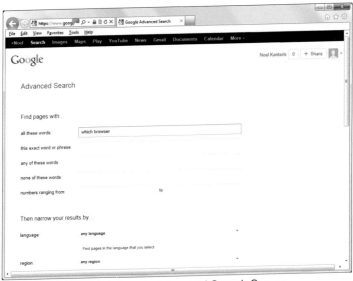

Fig. 1.6 A Google Advanced Search Screen.

From here you can specify whether all the words used in your search query are to be used in the search, perhaps exclude some words, search by region, etc.

Google's search results are integrated and can be made up of multiple content types, such as images, maps, videos, news, etc. It searches across all of these content sources, integrates and then ranks the results for the best answers. Fig. 1.7 on the next page shows results for the search query *birds* under Images, while Fig. 1.8 shows **YouTube** videos on the same subject. Each screen is obtained by first clicking Images then YouTube on the Google **Navigation** bar.

Fig. 1.7 A Google Search for Images of Birds.

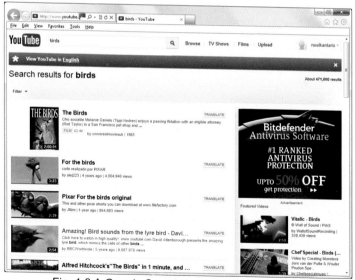

Fig. 1.8 A Google Search for Videos on YouTube.

Do watch the video of Australia's most amazing Lyre bird.

About Search Terms

With Google, choosing the right search terms is the key to finding the information you need. It is often better to use multiple search terms. If you're planning a vacation in Cornwall, you may do better searching for **vacation cornwall** than with the words by themselves. And if you are interested in fishing, then **vacation cornwall fishing** may produce even better results. Choose your search terms carefully as Google can only look for what you choose.

Google searches are **NOT** case sensitive. All letters, regardless of how you type them, will be understood as lower case, so there is no point using capitals.

By default, Google only returns pages that include all of your search terms, and the order in which the terms are typed will affect the search results. To restrict a search further, just include more terms.

Google ignores common words and characters such as "in" and "how", and single digits and letters, because they slow down a search without improving the results. If a common word is essential to getting the results you want, you can include it by putting a "+" sign in front of it, but make sure there is a space before the "+".

Another method for doing this is conducting a phrase search and putting quotation marks "" around two or more words. Common words in a phrase search, such as "where are you" are included in the search. Phrase searches are also effective when searching for specific phrases such as in names, song lyrics, quotations or poems.

I'm Feeling Lucky

You can force Google to go straight to what it considers the most relevant Web site for your query. To do this, enter your search terms on the Google home page as usual, but click the I'm Feeling Lucky link, as shown in Fig. 1.9 on the next page, instead of the normal Google **Search** button. The result is displayed in Fig. 1.10, also shown on the next page.

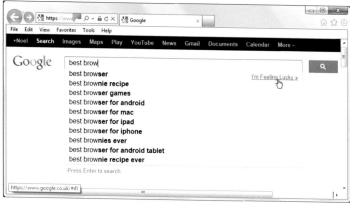

Fig. 1.9 About to Click the I'm Feeling Lucky Link.

Fig. 1.10 The I'm Feeling Lucky Screen Result.

Special Search Features

In addition to providing easy access to billions of Web pages, Google Web Search has some special features that not many people know about. With these, the feature result appears at the top of the list of Web page results.

Try typing ***things to do*** in Google's **Search** box of the Google's UK site. What displays immediately is a list similar to the one shown below.

Fig. 1.11 Some 'Things to do' in a Selection of UK Cities.

Clicking the link pointed to in Fig. 1.11, displays a colourful screen with a changing picture at the bottom half of the page, as shown in Fig. 1.12 below.

Fig. 1.12 Some 'Things to do' in Brighton.

Please bear in mind though, that Google is always in a state of flux. New features are added quite often and by the time you read this, there may be many more of them, or some might have disappeared!

Weather in Any Location

To see the weather for most UK towns and cities, type *weather* followed by the town name into a Google **Search** box and click the **Search** button. Sometimes a county or postcode is needed as well.

Fig. 1.13 Getting an Instant Weather Forecast.

Time in Any Location

To get the current time in most cities of the world, type in *time* and the name of the city, as I have shown in Fig. 1.14.

Fig. 1.14 Getting the Time in a Specified Location.

If you just type *time* you will get the current time for wherever you are.

You could also get a World clock by typing *world clock* in Google's **Search** box which displays Fig. 1.15.

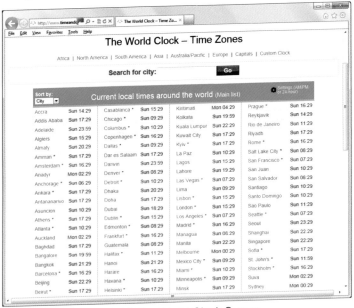

Fig. 1.15 The World Clock Screen.

Cinema in your Locality

If you want to go to the cinema, Google is the first place to look. Just type *cinema* followed by the name of its location into the Google **Search** box, and click the **Search** button. You should get a result similar to that shown in Fig. 1.16 on the next page, listing all the films in the specified location (city of Truro in our example). You even get a map of the location of the cinema!

To find details for one of the listed films, simply click on it to display all the nearby towns that this film is currently showing in, together with the starting times for each location as displayed in Fig. 1.17, also shown on the next page.

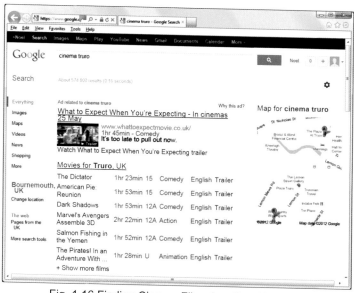

Fig. 1.16 Finding Cinema Films in a Specific Area.

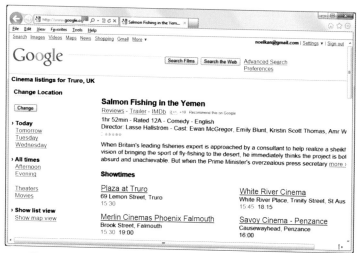

Fig. 1.17 Finding a Selected Cinema Film in your Locality.

Search results for a film include a star rating (out of 5), snippets from online reviews, as well as links to the full reviews themselves, and to trailers for the film, as shown in Fig. 1.18. More than enough information to plan your evening!

Fig. 1.18 Finding Reviews and Trailers.

Airline Travel Information

To check the flight status for domestic or international flights just type the details, such as *air southwest sz 103* into the search box and click on **Search**. This can be very useful if you have to meet an incoming flight.

Fig. 1.19 Finding Current Flight Information.

Google Q&A

Sometimes entering a simple question into Google, such as **'height of mount everest'** or **'when was david cameron born'** will come up with the answers:

Mount Everest, Elevation – 29,028 feet (8,848 m)
and
October 9, 1966

respectively.

Currency Conversion

Google has a built-in currency converter, so if you are going to Greece on vacation and want to take 1500 Euros with you, simply enter the words *1500 euros in pounds* into the **Search** box and click the **Search** button. Part of what displays on your screen is shown below.

Fig. 1.20 Currency Conversion.

If you don't know the currency of your target, just enter a simple search text into Google, like *egyptian currency to pounds*, and click the **Search** button. Again, part of what displays on your screen is shown below.

Fig. 1.21 Currency Conversion.

And to think that less than 50 years ago these two currencies were on par! That shows what inflation can do to the currency of a country in such a short time.

Local Business Searches

If you're looking for a store, restaurant, or other local business or service you can search for the category of business and the location and Google will return your information on the results page, with a map and contact information, as shown below for our search *Italian restaurants truro*. Sometimes you have to add the county as well as the town, to get this to work.

Fig. 1.22 Results of a Typical Local Business Search.

Maps

If you need a quick map to find a location or post code, just type in the name of the location, or post code, followed by '**map**' and Google will return a small map of the location.

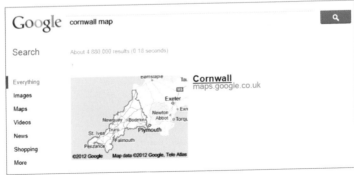

Fig. 1.23 Generating a Quick Map.

Clicking on the map will take you to a much more detailed version in Google **Maps**, which is described later in the book.

Sports Results

To see scores and schedules for sports teams type the team name or league name into the search box. If you are lucky this will work for your team.

Fig. 1.24 Finding Rapid Sports Results.

Dictionary

To get a quick definition for a word or phrase, simply type the word **define** followed by the word or phrase you want to know about.

Fig. 1.25 Using Google Search as a Dictionary.

Calculator

Google Web Search includes another special feature which I think deserves a small section of its own, the calculator. This does not have a front-end, you just type your maths problem straight into the search box and get instant answers. As long as you have your browser open to the Internet it is always just a click away. The calculator will even recognise words as well as numbers.

The entries *three times four plus three* gives the answer **fifteen**, while *3 times 4 plus 3*, or *3*4+3*, give the answer **15**.

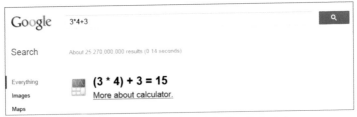

Fig. 1.26 Entering Numbers into the Calculator.

This very powerful feature lets you perform simple as well as complex calculations using Google's **Search** box. It can solve problems involving basic arithmetic, units of measure, conversions, and physical constants.

As well as text you can use the usual operators, **+** for addition, **−** for subtraction, ***** for multiplication, **/** for division, and **^** for exponentiation (raising to the power of). In Fig. 1.27 we show how trigonometric functions can very easily be used.

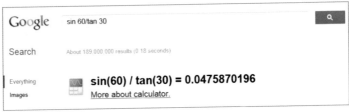

Fig. 1.27 Using Trigonometric Functions in the Calculator.

Making Conversions

One of the things that makes the Google calculator so useful for us is its ability to make conversions between types of units. As long as you label them, you can use mixed units in a query and even get your results converted to something else.

The terminology for conversions is:

(old units) in (new units)

The example in Fig. 1.28 below shows the use of automatic and forced conversions in the calculator.

Fig. 1.28 A Calculation Using Mixed Units

The above capability is really an excellent feature and we strongly recommend you experiment with it.

Google Search Restrictions

We have seen earlier how to use the **Images** search on the Google **Navigation** bar to obtain pictures of *birds*. You can use the same technique to obtain specific types of photos, icons, drawings and maps. This gives you access to millions of indexed pictures which are available for viewing.

In its search indexes Google analyses the text on the pages next to images, the captions and filenames of embedded images and other factors to make its image content selection for a search. Highest quality images are usually presented first in the results.

If the **Images** results page contains photographs 'with adult content' and that is not what you want, you can enable the **SafeSearch** filter, as follows:

To open the **SafeSearch** page, type in Google's address bar:

http://www.google.co.uk/preferences

which opens the page shown in Fig. 1.29 below.

Fig. 1.29 The SafeSearch Filters Page.

Use the slide to select one of three options:

No filtering   This turns off **SafeSearch** filtering completely. Depending on what you are searching for you may need to be fairly broad minded for this setting.

Moderate   Most explicit images are filtered out from an Images Search, but ordinary Web search results are not filtered. This is the default **SafeSearch** setting, which will be active until changed.

Strict   This applies **SafeSearch** filtering to all
                          your search results (both images
                          search and ordinary Web search).

Having made your selection, click the [Save] button at the
bottom of the screen, then the **Lock SafeSearch** link to open
a further page as shown in Fig. 1.30 below.

Fig. 1.30 The SafeSearch Lock Page.

You need to **Sign in** to complete any changes you have
made. Having done so, click the [Lock SafeSearch] button to be
found on the next displayed screen. This, in turn, displays a
further screen, as shown in Fig. 1.31 on the next page.

What is shown in Fig. 1.31 is the locking in progress, of
SafeSearch process across all Google domains.

Fig. 1.31 The SafeSearch Lock Process.

The default setting (**Moderate**) works well with us, but with some searches the **Strict** option may be needed. It's sometimes interesting to click between the three options to see how Google image 'censoring' works. At the end of the day, of course, the choice is yours.

No filtering can ever be perfectly accurate. If you have **Strict SafeSearch** activated and still find sites containing offensive content in your results, you can click the Report these images link (you'll find this link if you scroll down in Fig. 1.29). You can then tick the images you object to and hopefully Google will remove them from future results.

Have fun looking through the enormous volume of images available, but don't forget to come back and finish reading this book!

The **SafeSearch** feature may be useful if you want to restrict what your grandchildren are able to view, if you let them use your computer!

2

Google Calendar & Mail

Perhaps you find it difficult and troublesome keeping an ordinary diary up to date. If that is the case, then try doing it online instead. Google Calendar is a free Web-based calendar (or diary) application that lets you keep track of all your important events and appointments online. It works in a Web browser (such as Microsoft Internet Explorer, Google Chrome or Firefox), in which both JavaScript and cookies have been enabled. Then no matter where you are, once you are online, you will have access to your diary.

To create a new calendar from scratch, or to import an existing one, you need to start Google in your browser and click on the **Calendar** link on the Google **Navigation** bar pointed to in Fig. 2.1 below. If this link is not visible on your Google **Navigation** bar, click the More link and select Calendar from the drop-down menu.

Fig. 2.1 Opening the Calendar in Internet Explorer.

If you already have a Google account and you are signed in, this opens the **Calendar** screen. If not, it opens the 'Sign in' window, (Fig. 2.2 below), in which you can sign in to your Google Account if you have one, or click the [SIGN UP] button to create an account if you don't.

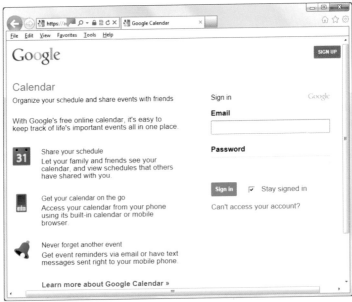

Fig. 2.2 Signing in to the Google Account.

Creating a Google Account

You can't use Google Calendar (or Mail) unless you have an account with Google, so if you don't have an account click the [SIGN UP] button, fill out the required fields in the window that opens, click the **I agree to the Google Terms** box and click the [Create my account.] button. This procedure is necessary because the contents of your calendar will be kept online, or 'in the clouds' by Google. That way you can access them from anywhere by just signing in.

To check that the e-mail address you associated with your account is correct, Google sends a message to it. So check your e-mail for this verification message. Open the message and click on the link provided to activate your Google Account. That's it done, you now have a Google account which you can also use for any of Google's online applications, such as Gmail, Blogs, Reader, etc.

When you first sign in to Google **Calendar** a window similar to ours in Fig. 2.3 opens.

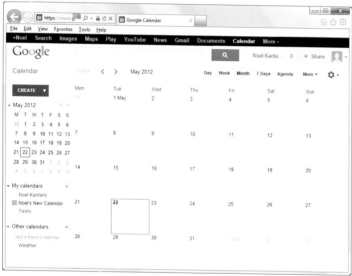

Fig. 2.3 A Newly Opened Google Calendar.

To illustrate the above, a 'New Calendar' was created, even though a fully functional calendar already exists for us. Note the box at the bottom left of the screen; if you click it the **Weather** is added to your calendar and the box turns pink.

Further clicking on **Other calendars**, displays a menu with options as shown in Fig. 2.4.

Fig. 2.4 Options.

Clicking on the **Browse Interesting Calendars** menu option reveals an incredible choice of further additions. We selected **Holidays**, then scrolled down to **UK Holidays** and clicked **Subscribe**, as shown in Fig. 2.5 below.

Fig. 2.5 Selecting the Type of Holidays to Display in a Calendar.

The calendar now should look similar to the one displayed in Fig. 2.6 below.

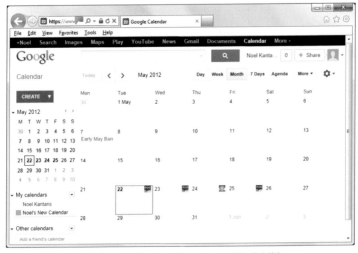

Fig. 2.6 A New Google Calendar with Additions.

The thumbnails at the top right of each day informs you what the weather is likely to be from today onwards – rather good!

Calendar Views

There are five default ways to view your calendar which you control from the tabs on the bar above the work area.

Fig. 2.7 Controlling the Calendar Views.

As shown, you can view just a day, a week, a month, 7 days, or the Agenda which is a text listing of your entries. To move through the calendar (by a month in this example), click the **Back** ‹ or **Forward** › buttons. The quick way to return to the current period (coloured pale blue) is to click the Today button.

Adding Events

There are several ways to add entries (Events) to a Google calendar. The easiest is to click the appropriate date/time slot single-click the working area to open a 'bubble box' similar to that of Fig. 2.8, and simply type in the details for the entry, then click the down-arrow of the **Create event** button shown in Fig. 2.9 below.

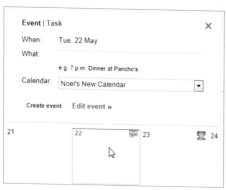

Fig. 2.8 Creating an Event.

To add more to the Event click the **Edit event >>** link to open the screen shown in Fig. 2.10 on the next page.

Fig. 2.9 Creating a Quick Event.

Fig. 2.10 Adding and Changing Details to a Calendar Event.

Here you can enter or change the date, starting time, end time, location, and description of your event by replacing the default 'Untitled event'. This very screen will also open had you double-clicked on a date/time slot, while Fig. 2.8 was displayed using a single-click.

If you want to be reminded of the event, use the **Add a reminder** link. You can choose to be reminded by e-mail or a pop-up message on your computer screen. When you are finished click the **Save** button, give it a name (I called it 'Meeting with Fred') and you can then see the flag that appears at the top of the **Calendar** screen, as shown below.

Added Meeting with Fred on Tue 22 May 2012. Undo

Repeating Events

For repeating events such as birthdays, anniversaries or regular meetings, click in the **Repeat** check box, select when you want the event repeated and then how often in the following entry box.

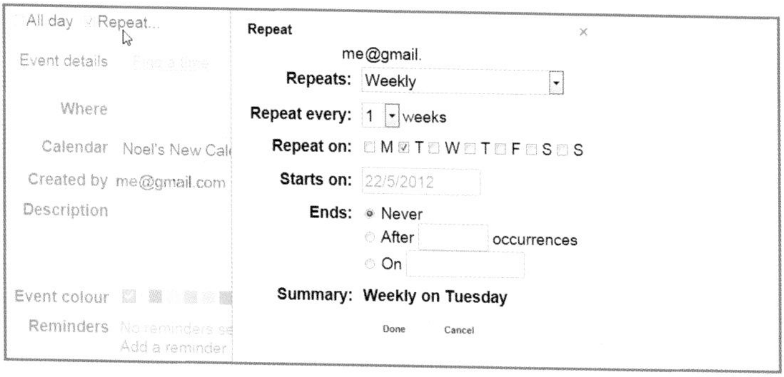

Fig. 2.11 Repeating Events.

This is probably a good time to get out your family details and enter all the birthdays and anniversaries into your new calendar, changing the **Repeats** box to *Yearly*. If you set for e-mail reminders to be sent to you a few days before each one occurs you should never be caught short again. I certainly find any help like this to be indispensable these days, as my memory is not what it used to be!

Customising a Calendar

To customise your calendar, click the **Settings** icon at the top right of the screen pointed to in Fig. 2.12 below.

Fig. 2.12 The Settings Icon.

As you can see, from the drop-down **Settings** menu, shown

here in Fig. 2.13, you can select one of three **Display Density** options, or select **Settings**, **Help**, or **Labs** (a testing ground for experimental features). Selecting **Settings** from the drop-down menu, displays the screen shown in Fig. 2.14 below.

In the **General** tab, set your preferences for **Language**, **Current time zone**, **Date** and **Time format**, **Default meeting length**, etc., as shown below. To apply your new preferences just click the **Save** button near the top of the screen.

Fig. 2.13 The Settings Drop-down Menu.

Fig. 2.14 Part of a Google Calendar Settings Screen.

Creating a Calendar

You can have multiple calendars with Google **Calendar**. This can be useful if you want to include other family members, or monitor a specific part of your life. I have separate calendars to keep track of some of my fixed rate financial bonds. To open a new calendar click the down-arrow next to the **My calendars** box, shown on the bottom left in Fig. 2.3, select **Create new Calendar** from the drop-down menu, give it a name and description and press the **Create Calendar** button near the top of the displayed screen.

Calendar Colours

Every calendar you create is given a different colour and its entries appear in that colour, as shown for the example in Fig. 2.15.

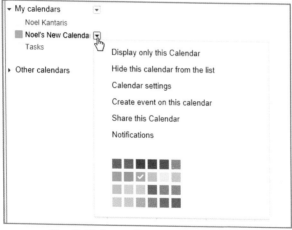

Fig. 2.15 Controlling Calendar Colours.

To choose a different colour for one of the calendars, click the down-arrow against it and select a new colour from the options at the bottom of the displayed menu. This drop-down menu also gives you options to display and hide the calendar, change its settings, create an event on this calendar and you can even choose to share the calendar with other people.

When a calendar listed in the **My calendars** is currently the selected calendar, its box is shown as a solid colour and all its entries will display in the main calendar working area. If you have a lot of different calendars this can get somewhat confusing if they are all active, as shown in Fig. 2.16.

Fig. 2.16 Two Active Calendars.

This doesn't pose any problem though; when you don't want a particular one to show you can just click its entry in the **My calendars** list. This will 'switch it off', remove the colour from its square, and temporarily remove its entries from the display. The **Tasks** option in the list, opens or closes a new **Tasks** panel for you to make and maintain a **Tasks** (or To Do) list.

Searching Calendars

As you might expect with Google you can search for items or events in either your own calendars or in other Public calendars. To do so, type a query in the text box at the top of the calendar screen and click the **Search My Calendars** button.

To see the type of queries you can use and where you can search, click the down arrow to the right of the **Search** box, to open the screen shown here in Fig. 2.17.

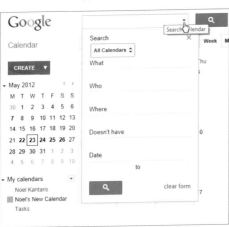

Fig. 2.17 Calendar Search Options.

Google Mail

Google **Mail**, or **Gmail** as it is now called, is a Web application that allows you to create, send and receive e-mail messages in your browser, and to store them freely and securely on Google's data sites. Your e-mail messages are then accessible to you at any time from anywhere. **Gmail** has some useful features:

- It lets you search your e-mail messages quickly and efficiently provided you archive rather than delete them.

- There is no need to delete messages as Google allows you around 10.25 GB of online storage space.

- It filters all your messages for spam so you shouldn't have to worry on that score.

You can open **Gmail** from any Google page by clicking the Gmail link on the Google **Navigation Bar** (see Fig. 2.1). If necessary, 'Sign in' if you already have a Google account, or 'Sign up' if not, as described earlier in the Chapter. The first time we did this the following message screen displayed.

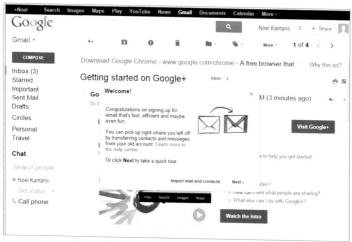

Fig. 2.18 Google Mail's Introductory Page.

In Fig. 2.18 you are given the opportunity to transfer your contacts and messages from a previous account, take a quick tour of the services offered, customise your account, etc. After reading this information, and acting on what is appropriate, click the **Inbox** on the left of the screen to open the welcoming e-mail messages from the **Gmail** team.

Bear in mind that Google changes very often what appears on your screen, so don't be surprised if what you see differs from what we describe here. What displays on my screen is shown in Fig. 2.19 below.

Fig. 2.19 The Gmail Window.

You really should open each one of these by just clicking it. When you have finished with a message click the **Back to Inbox** button, to be found at the top of the screen in Fig. 2.18 on the previous page and also shown here with its label showing, to go to the next message.

Spend a while reading what they have to say and follow the links in each. You should then be well set up for customising and using **Gmail**. You can also use the **Chat** button at the bottom of the screen to chat to friends, or the adjacent button (the one with the 3 dots) to invite a friend to join **Gmail**.

The Gmail Window

Apart from being Web based, the main difference between **Gmail** and other e-mail programs like the **Windows Live Mail** and **Outlook**, is that it automatically groups all your e-mail messages with their answers into 'Conversations' so you don't have to organise your e-mail messages into different folders.

Thus, provided you don't delete any e-mails (but archive them instead), it is easy to find any e-mail you sent and it is then displayed together with all the answers you received on the subject. What a fantastic concept! Also, a single conversation can have several labels, so if a conversation covers more than one topic, you can retrieve it with any of the labels that you have applied to it.

The other program options (Fig. 2.20) available on the left of the Gmail window, include:

Fig. 2.20 Gmail Program Options.

Gmail – Left-clicking the arrowhead, pointed to, displays a drop-down menu with options for accessing mail, contacts, or tasks to remember.

Fig. 2.21 Gmail Options.

Compose – Opens a new message form for you to type a new e-mail.

Inbox – Returns a list of received e-mail messages. The number in brackets shows the number of unread messages.

Starred – Displays a list of your starred e-mail messages. To star a message, click the light blue star beside any message or conversation to give it a special status.

Circles – Displays a list of friends in your inner circle.

Important – Clicking a message in the **Inbox**, as shown in Fig. 2.22, marks it as **Important** and places a copy of it in the **Important** folder.

Fig. 2.22 Marking a Message in the Inbox as Important.

Sent Mail – Displays a list of messages you have sent.

Drafts – Displays a list of messages you have not sent.

More/Less – Opens/Closes more options (shown open in Fig. 2.20), including:

Chats – Displays a history of your chats. **Gmail**'s chat features allow you to make free voice calls by connecting you to the **Google Talk** network.

All Mail – Displays all the messages you have received, sent, or archived, but not those you have deleted.

Spam – Displays all e-mail messages that have been marked as spam.

Bin – Displays all the e-mail messages you have deleted. Selecting a message (click the box to the left of it), displays the **Delete forever** button at the top of the screen and clicking it removes the messages permanently. Messages left in the **Bin** for more than 30 days are deleted automatically.

Contacts

The **Gmail Contacts** list allows you to store addresses, phone numbers, e-mail addresses and notes for all your contacts. Whenever you send an e-mail to someone, their e-mail address is added to your **Contacts** list automatically. By clicking on a contact you can view more information and all your conversations with that person. You can add a new contact manually by clicking the Contacts link, then the **New contact** button and entering the contacts details.

Fig. 2.23 Gmail Program Options.

Composing a New Message

To compose and send a new message, click the COMPOSE button. This opens the window shown in Fig. 2.24.

In the **To:** box you type the recipient's e-mail address. If the person is in your **Contacts** list, then typing the first letter of a name will list all addresses starting with that letter. All you have to do is choose the appropriate one.

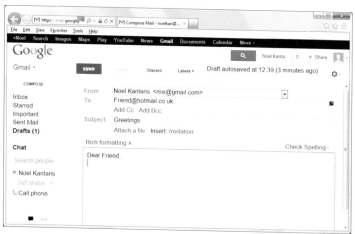

Fig. 2.24 Composing a New Message.

The best way to test out any unfamiliar e-mail features is to send a test message to your own e-mail address, which also saves wasting somebody else's time.

Next, type a title for the message in the **Subject:** box. The text in this subject field will form a header for the message when it is received, so it helps to show in a few words what the message is about.

Finally, type your message and click the SEND button.

Message Formatting

Gmail provides quite sophisticated formatting options for an e-mail editor.

Fig. 2.25 Turning on Formatting Features.

To turn on the formatting features of the **Gmail** editor, click the **Rich formatting** link pointed to above in Fig. 2.25, which opens the screen below.

Fig. 2.26 The Displayed Formatting Features.

All the formatting features are self-explanatory. If you hover the mouse pointer over an icon on the **Format** bar, a bubble message opens telling you of its function. Left-clicking one such icon, either actions the formatting or displays further options to choose from.

You should be able to prepare some very easily readable e-mail messages with these features, particularly if you use the **Check Spelling** link pointed to in Fig. 2.26 above.

Using E-mail Attachments

If you want to include an attachment with your main e-mail message, you simply click the **Attach a file** link, under the **Subject** box, which opens a separate window displaying your Desktop, from which you can navigate to the file you want to attach. This could be a document, a photo, or indeed a video.

When you receive a message with an attachment, it displays with a paper clip to the right, as pointed to in Fig. 2.27 below. Hovering the mouse pointer on the paper clip displays the name and type of the attachment. In our example the attachment contains an image **.JPG** file.

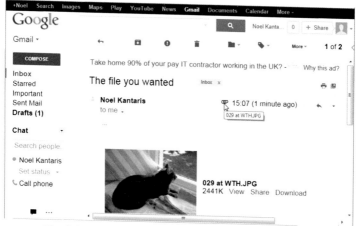

Fig. 2.27 A Received Message with an Attached File.

Right-clicking the attachment displays a choice of options, the main ones being to save the attachment on your hard disc, e-mail it to a friend, or print it.

Now, we don't know how you feel about the ever changing advert appearing at the top of your the e-mail screen, but we are finding it very annoying indeed. So let us do something about it.

If you click on the Why this add? link at the right of the advert, it opens a bubble that tells you that the advert is based on the e-mail content in your **Inbox** – well, it doesn't for us! At the same time it provides you with the Ads Preferences Manager link which you should follow. You are asked to sign in again, then the **Ad Preferences** screen is displayed. From here you can block specific advertisers, or you can click the Opt out link on the left of the screen to remove the adverts appearing on the right of the screen, but not the one that annoys us at the top!

Managing Received E-mail Messages

When you receive an e-mail and left-click it to open it (so you can read its content), the following bar appears at the top of the screen.

Fig. 2.28 The Displayed Formatting Features.

The function of these buttons (going from left to right), is: Back to Inbox, Archive, Report spam, Delete, Move to, Labels, and More. The last three have further menu options which can be accessed by clicking the small arrowhead next to them.

To keep your **Inbox** tidy, messages can be given labels by first opening them, then clicking the **Label** ❧· button. Labels can help categorise messages, for example as work, family, etc., and are better than folders because they have the added advantage that you can allocate more than one label to an e-mail if it is from, say, a family member about a work project. Such an e-mail will be listed if you are searching for 'work' or 'family'.

Further, you can archive e-mail messages by first selecting them by clicking the check boxes ☑ to the left of each message, then using the **Archive** ▣ button. Archiving removes messages from your **Inbox** and moves them into your **All Mail** storage.

If someone responds to a message that has been archived, the message and its corresponding conversations will reappear in your **Inbox**. Archived messages can be found by clicking the All Mail link below the **Inbox** (if not visible, click the More link first). They can also be found by either clicking and selecting an appropriate label, or searching for them.

* * *

Both Google **Calendar** and Google **Mail** have many more features which we are sure you will be able to explore for yourself. Good luck!

3

Google News & Finance

Google News

 These days every newspaper and other news source has a Web site showing a continuously updated online version of its news and story contents. We all like to know what is happening and where.

Google goes one step further, it 'crawls' these news sites continuously, indexes their contents and presents a summary of the news as it happens in over 70 regional editions of Google **News**, including News UK shown below.

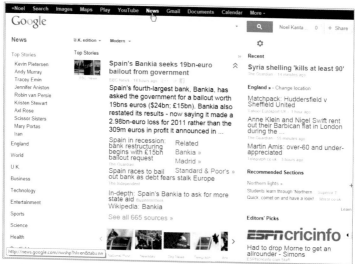

Fig. 3.1 The Top Stories Section of a Google News UK Page.

To access Google **News** just click on the **News** link at the top of the screen on the Google **Navigation** bar.

To change between the different international versions of **News** use the drop-down menu in the top-left of the window, (showing **UK** in Fig. 3.1).

Google News Layout

You can select the way news is displayed on your screen by clicking the down-arrow pointed to here on the left. The standard, or default, Google **News** page is called **Modern** and consists of the Top Stories section. Other page views are shown in Fig. 3.2 below.

Fig. 3.2 Options for News Page Layout.

These page views are available in all regional editions of Google News and are customisable. Other sections are listed on the left of the Google **News** screen, and are shown here in Fig. 3.3.

The Top Stories section shows the most active stories throughout all sites, while the Spotlight section shows the most popular stories in the Google **News** edition actually being viewed.

England
World
U.K.
Business
Technology
Entertainment
Sports
Science
Health
Spotlight

Fig. 3.3 News Sections.

Google **News** is 'untouched by human hand' as the stories, headlines and photos you see on it are selected entirely by computer algorithms, based on factors like how often and where a story appears online. The grouping and ranking of stories depends on such things as titles, text, and publication time.

The standard Google **News** pages include news items published in the last 30 days, but Google doesn't throw the indexed data away then. It is included in the Google **News** **Archive** looked at later in this chapter.

News Clusters

Google groups **News** articles about the same story together, as shown in Fig. 3.4, and calls these groups, clusters. This makes it easy to read versions of the same news from different sources, or see how a story evolves over time. Clicking on the link to See all 1,618 sources (in our example) about a story will open a listing of the whole cluster.

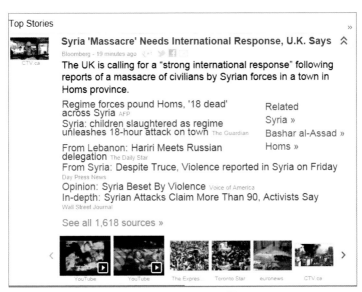

Fig. 3.4 A Typical News Cluster.

How fresh a news story is, is shown by how long ago it was posted, e.g., **19 minutes ago** for the first one in Fig. 3.4 above. You click on the title to display the article, or one of the other links that display below it.

If you hover the mouse pointer over an image a box opens below with text details about the news item, as shown here. You can click links in this floating box to go to the news story. You can also get more news on the same topic by clicking one of the links listed below **Related** in Fig. 3.4.

Searching Google News

You search Google **News** by entering your query and clicking on the **Search** button. A search for *London*, for example, displays several million results which by default are sorted by relevance to your search terms for that date and time. The first few items found for our search criteria is shown in Fig. 3.5.

Fig. 3.5 Searching for Specific News.

Note the list on the left of the screen. It includes Images, Maps, and Videos links. If you click the Images link, you get some pleasant images of London, as shown in Fig. 3.6 on the next page.

To see related image searches, click one of the links that appear at the top of the displayed images. To see relevant videos, click the Videos link on the left of the screen. There are videos from the BBC News, such as 'On board London's air ambulance', 'London skyscrapers that were planned', 'London's new cable car tested', etc., at least for that date and time. However, what is offered changes quite frequently, so don't be surprised if your get different results.

Fig. 3.6 Images Search for London News.

You can also limit a search to a specific country. For example, searching for images of **food restaurants in London Ontario** displays the screen shown in Fig. 3.7.

Fig. 3.7 Images Search for London Ontario (Canada).

Searching News Archives

Google's **News Archive Search** gives an easy way to search and explore historical archives, such as major newspapers, magazines, news archives and legal archives. Remember that Google stores any news over 30 days old in its **News Archives** database.

You can search for events, people or ideas and see how they have been described over time. Search results include content that is freely accessible to everyone and also that which requires a fee to access.

As an example of this feature, type *archives* in the Google **News** home page, then click the Archives link that appears at the end of the **Search** list. Next, typing *armenian genocide* in the Google **Search** box, displays the screen in Fig. 3.8.

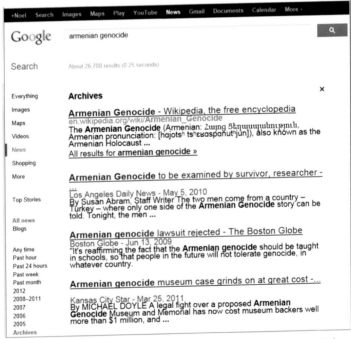

Fig. 3.8 News Archive Search Results for 'Armenian Genocide'.

Google Finance

If you have a financial or business interest in company stocks and shares, mutual funds and international currency rates, then Google **Finance** will be useful to you. If not, you can probably skip the rest of this chapter. Google **Finance** offers an easy way to search for share prices, mutual fund details, and financial information on publicly listed companies. All the things pensions are made up from!

To access the Google **Finance** page, simply click the More option on the Google **Navigation** bar to open the drop-down menu shown in Fig. 3.9 below, then click the Finance link to display the screen from Google UK, shown in Fig. 3.10 on the next page.

Fig. 3.9 The Google News Search Result for Finance.

Fig. 3.10 Part of the Google UK Finance Page.

The opening page should look similar to the one above, but obviously with different content. The top section of the page, consists of the usual Google **Navigation** bar, with a list of links under **Finance** on the left, such as Markets, News, and Portfolios. If you have obtained any quotes, these will be listed under **Recent Quotes**. Do scroll down, there is more information on **Currency**, **Trends** and **Sector summary**.

You use this page to search for prices of stock market companies, or mutual funds, using either their names or their ticker symbols. Google have been very clever here with their *Autosuggest* feature. As you type in the first part of a name a list instantly appears which suggests what you might be looking for, as shown in Fig. 3.11 on the next page. You just click the option you want in the list, the ticker symbol is automatically placed in the **Get quotes** box, and the home page changes to a detailed page of data on the security you searched for, as shown in Fig. 3.12 also on the next page.

sai
SBRY	J **Sai**nsbury plc
SAI	**SAI**C, Inc.
600104	**SAI**C Motor Corporation Limited
SGO	Compagnie de **Sai**nt Gobain SA
SPM	**Sai**pem SpA
SPMR	**Sai**pem SpA
SAIL	Steel Authority of India Limited
JSAIY	J **Sai**nsbury plc (ADR)

Fig. 3.11 Autosuggestion.

Market Summary

This gives an overview of the current UK financial situation, with access to the main news story on the left, summarises the main current FTSE indices, and shows the main currency exchange rates.

Fig. 3.12 SBRY Performance and FTSE 100 Index Charts.

This is but a fraction of the information displayed on your screen on the subject. Below the data shown above, the performance of **Related companies** is displayed, as shown in Fig. 3.13 on the next page, and below that is **Description** of the company in question and a list of **Offices and Directors** – enough reading to form a learned opinion!

	Company name	Price	Change	Valuation Chg %	d | m | y	Mkt Cap
	Related companies					
	Show: Most Recent Annual				Add or remove columns	
SBRY	J Sainsbury plc	293.45	-2.05	-0.69%		5,526.77M
TSCO	Tesco PLC	305.67	-3.88	-1.25%		24,561.41M
WMK	Weis Markets, Inc.	44.07	-0.19	-0.43%		1,185.41M
RAL	Rallye SA	23.73	-0.47	-1.94%		1,099.76M
WFM	Whole Foods Marke…	87.27	+0.85	0.98%		16,019.62M
DELB	Delhaize Group	31.32	-0.16	-0.51%		3,159.82M
AH	Koninklijke Ahold…	9.58	-0.07	-0.72%		10,158.23M
MRW	Wm. Morrison Supe…	274.30	+1.30	0.48%		6,803.00M
CBD	Companhia Brasile…	40.29	+1.50	3.87%		10,484.20M
KR	The Kroger Co.	22.41	+0.26	1.17%		12,571.38M
MGNT	OJSC Magnit					

Sector: Services > Industry: Retail
(Grocery)

More from Revere Data »

Fig. 3.13 Performance of Related Companies.

Market News

News stories on Google **Finance** are accessed by clicking the **News** link under the **Markets** heading (see Fig. 3.10) The home page shows the **Top stories** for the **Market** generally, news for **Portfolio related** shares if you have a portfolio of shares open, or **Recent quote related** news if you don't.

Tracking Currencies

Google **Finance** offers data on how leading currencies are performing against each other. You'll find a list of currencies on the home page (scroll down on the screen shown in Fig. 3.10), to see a list similar to the one shown here in Fig. 3.14.

Clicking on a link such as **GBP/EUR**, displays a page with a history chart, as shown in Fig. 3.15 on the next page, and relevant news, and current exchange rates for this and the other main financial currencies.

Currencies		
GBP/USD	1.5706	+0.0049 (0.31%)
GBP/EUR	1.2526	+0.0018 (0.14%)
GBP/JPY	124.8470	+0.1550 (0.12%)
GBP/HKD	12.1927	+0.0386 (0.32%)
GBP/CNY	9.9655	+0.0328 (0.33%)
GBP/AUD	1.5952	-0.0077 (-0.48%)

Fig. 3.14 Major Currency Exchange Rates.

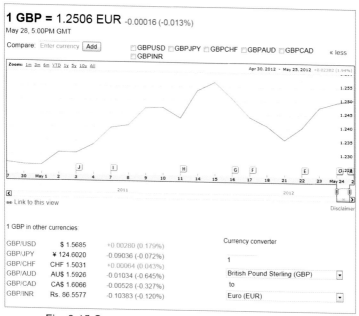

Fig. 3.15 Currency Exchange Rates and Conversion.

There is also a very useful currency converter at the bottom of the page, shown in Fig. 3.15 above, but well to the right of the screen. I placed this where it is shown above for convenience, making it easier to display. You can use the down-arrowheads to select from a list of currencies.

Your Own Portfolios

Google Finance lets you create and maintain portfolios of shares and mutual funds. This helps you to keep track of your investments and instantly know their actual value. It also gives you access to relevant financial information such as news and company management details.

To create a portfolio you need to be signed in to a Google **Account**. Then you can click the Portfolios link on the left of the Google **Finance** page, as shown on the next page.

Fig. 3.16 Creating a First Portfolio.

From here you just plough straight in and add the transactions you want to show by clicking the **Add transaction data** link. If you want Google **Finance** to work out total values, etc., of your portfolio, each transaction needs details of at least the number of **Shares** and their **Price** (enter this in pence, not pounds). If you just want to watch a share, you can leave these blank.

The **Edit portfolio** option lets you change the sorting of entries within a portfolio, or quickly add or delete portfolio entries, by adding or deleting their ticker names.

The **Edit transactions** option lets you add or edit data for specific transactions in the portfolio, such as **Date**, number of **Shares**, **Price** paid for a security, the **Commission** paid or **Notes**. To finalise any changes made, you have to click the **Save changes** button.

To delete a portfolio from your account click the **Delete Portfolio** link and then click the **OK** button to 'Permanently delete this portfolio and all transactions in it' on the displayed dialogue box.

* * *

Good luck using Google Finance, I certainly enjoy it. But lets hope you have more 'luck' with your investments than I have managed so far! I simply blame the state of the International market rather than my judgement!

4

Google Plus & Google Drive

Google has two main applications, under Google **Plus** (**+**), that you can use for sharing, viewing and handling digital **Photos** and **Videos**. They are both to be found in the menu that displays when you click the More link on the Google **Navigation** bar as shown here. Do forgive the three pointing hands on our display – it helps us to point you in the right direction! You, of course, will only see one hand at a time.

Google Photos

Going back to the Google **Navigation** bar, click the More link then the Photos link to open the screen shown in Fig. 4.1 below.

Fig. 4.1 The Photos Opening Screen.

Note that at the top of the screen, the Google colourful logo now has a **+** sign next to it. It is the new Google **Plus** utility, whose applications are mostly aimed towards mobile devices such as smart phones and tablets, and what is perceived to be their preferred use by the younger generation; 'Sharing', 'Chatting' and creating 'Hangouts'. But don't despair, we are dealing with only photos here!

On the left of the screen (Fig. 4.1), hovering the mouse pointer over the **Photos** link, as shown in Fig. 4.2, displays

two further links; **From phone**, and **Albums**. You should first select one of these two links, then having done so, click the **ADD PHOTOS** link.

Fig. 4.2 Photo Links.

If you follow the **From phone** link, and try to upload photos from your phone, you are asked to download an App to allow you to carry on. This displays the screen shown in Fig. 4.3 below.

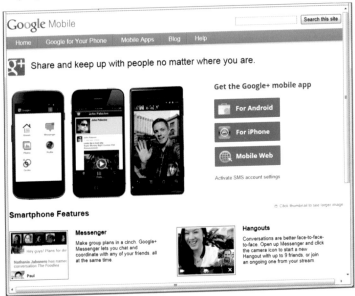

Fig. 4.3 The Photos Opening Screen.

As you can see, Google caters for only two types of smart phones; **Android** driven ones and Apple's **iPhone**. These Apps, when downloaded and installed, allow you to send photos from your phone directly to your friends.

The third option on the screen in Fig. 4.3 is Mobile Web. This allows you to select friends or family that use Google **+** to join your circles so you can enjoy common experiences.

The last link in Fig. 4.2, Albums, assumes you have already uploaded an album with photos on Google **+**. If you haven't, it offers the Upload photos now link which, when clicked, displays the screen in Fig. 4.4

Fig. 4.4 Selecting Photos from a PC.

From here you can browse to locate and select the photos you want to upload and share. The screen in Fig. 4.5 below, shows the uploading of an additional photo to our already uploaded selection of photos.

Fig. 4.5 Uploading an Additional Photo.

You can also create an album, add a comment, and select the friend or circle of friends and family you want to share these photos with. These friends must be members of Google **+** if they are going to benefit in sharing your photos.

In Fig. 4.6 below, you can lock the album, and select to share it with the chosen few via an e-mail link. Finally click the ![Save] button to complete the operation.

Fig. 4.6 Sharing Photos on Google **+**.

Editing Photos

In Fig. 4.7 we show a photo that we uploaded in a separate album, but it is rather dark, having taken it in semi-darkness without a flash, and needs editing. Clicking first the album, then the photo in the album, opens the screen below.

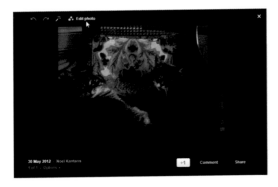

Fig. 4.7 Photo
Needing Editing.

Clicking the **Edit photo** button at the top of the screen in Fig. 4.7, opens the photo editor shown below.

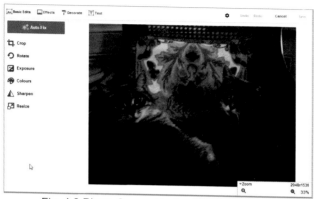

Fig. 4.8 Photo Opened in the Google **+** Editor.

Google **+** provides an array of editing tools for just such eventuality. You can **Auto-Fix** the photo, **Rotate** it, etc., all available under the **Basic Edits** menu option. We first used the **Auto-Fix**, then clicked the **Effects** menu option, selected the **Sun-Aged** and set fading to 70%, as shown in Fig. 4.9.

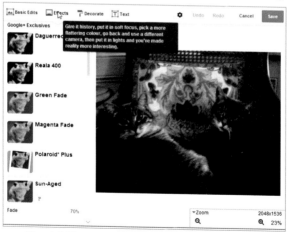

Fig. 4.9 The Edited Photo in the Google **+** Editor.

Quite an improvement, we think. We leave it to you to play with the various editing options. When satisfied click ▥ .

Google Videos

In the Google **Navigation** bar, click the More link then the Video link from the drop-down menu, to open the screen shown in Fig. 4.10 below.

Fig. 4.10 The Google Video Screen.

To see the screen as displayed above, you need to click the Share link followed by the Add video link. Clicking the Upload video link, displays the screen in Fig. 4.11 below.

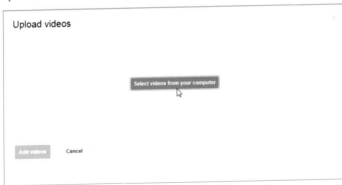

Fig. 4.11 Selecting a Video to Upload.

Next, click on the **Select video from your computer** button, browse to where you keep your videos and select one.

While a video is being uploaded, the following screen shown in Fig. 4.12, is displayed.

Fig. 4.12 Processing an Uploaded Video.

From here you can use the Upload more link to upload additional videos from your computer. Once the video processing has finished, you can have a look at the video for yourself, as shown in Fig. 4.13, to make sure you approve of the result, before inviting other people to look at it.

Fig. 4.13 Watching an Uploaded Video.

When satisfied that all is as it should be, click the **Add videos** button to add the names of friends and family that you would like to share the uploaded video with, as shown in Fig. 4.14 on the next page.

Fig. 4.14 Adding Friends to Share.

Fig. 4.15 Viewing Videos and Photos.

Fig. 4.16 Deleting a Video.

If you want to see your uploaded video, then you must return to the More, Photos link, as the Video link is only used to upload more videos which are treated by Google as photos.

So, now clicking the Photos link, and clicking the Albums button, displays the screen in Fig. 4.15.

Should you want to delete a video, click on it to start it, then click the Options link pointed to in Fig. 4.16, and from the displayed menu click the Delete Video option.

We leave it to you to explore all the capabilities of videos which are rather too many to include in this book.

We must warn you though, that you will not find uploaded photos and videos in your Google Drive, discussed next. The space on Google Drive is reserved for your personal documents and photos so that you can have them available wherever you are; it is not for the shared photos and videos which are kept in Google +.

Google Drive

 In the old days (actually less than 4 weeks since beginning this book), files kept on Google were held in Google **Documents** (see the Google **Navigation** bar in Fig. 1.2). By today, everything you had in Google **Documents** has been transferred to Google **Drive**.

If you never had any files in Google **Documents**, you'll need to create your own space in the cloud by typing:

www.drive.google.com

in the address box of your Web browser, which will display the screen shown in Fig. 4.17 below. The **.com** at the end of the above URL is important, as Google **Drive** is held there and not in Google's UK address.

Google **Drive** is a space you can use so that you can hold and access all your files from wherever you happen to be in the world at the time, not just from your own PC as was the case with Google **Documents**. Initially you are given 5 GB of free space to hold your files, but if you need more, you can purchase it for a small monthly fee ($2.50 for 25 GB).

Fig. 4.17 Creating your Own Google Drive.

To use Google **Drive** on any of your devices, whether a PC, an Apple computer, a tablet or a smart phone, you must first download an App on that device, as shown in Fig. 4.17.

It is important that you install Google **Drive** on all the devices you own. Changing any file from any device, automatically updates those changes to your Google **Drive** – as it synchronises uploaded files with all your devices.

As we own a PC, we clicked the **Download Google Drive for PC** button which displayed the screen in Fig. 4.18.

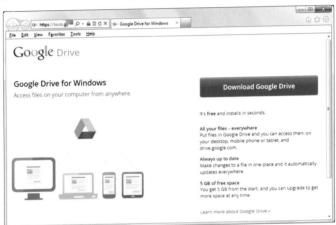

Fig. 4.18 Downloading Google Drive for Windows.

It took less that 10 seconds to download and install Google **Drive**. In the final installation screen, you are asked to create a password which you will need to access your files on your Google **Drive** in the future from any of your devices.

Perhaps now is the time to download the appropriate Apps on your other devices, if you have any, so you can fully test and appreciate the whole system later.

Remember, that just like before, when **Docs** were held in Google **Documents**, files held in Google **Drive** (whether word processed documents, spreadsheets, or presentations), can be created or edited online. The difference between the two is that now you can access and edit these files on any of your devices from wherever you happen to be.

In what follows, we will discuss the organisation of files already held on Google **Drive**, before discussing how to upload new files and how to synchronise and edited them.

Files Already on Google Drive

If you have used Google **Documents** before, your files would have been transferred to the new Google **Drive**. It is a good idea, therefore, to look at these files individually and delete any that are of no use to you anymore, as these files are automatically synchronised to your computer and other devices and count as part of your **Drive** space allocation.

To delete unwanted files on Google **Drive**, click the square to the left of the file you want to remove, to check it, then click the **Remove** button pointed to in Fig. 4.19.

Fig. 4.19 Deleting Unwanted Files from Google Drive.

If you want to remove all the old files on Google **Drive**, simply check the square to the left of the **TITLE** and click on the **Remove** button which only appears when you check the box.

Fig. 4.20 Files in Bin.

Deleted files on your Goggle **Drive** are kept in the **Bin**, but are still counted as part of your **Drive** space quota. It is, therefore, a good idea to 'delete them forever', if you don't need them.

Uploading Files on Google Drive

To start with a clean slate, we 'removed' all the files held in **My Drive** and 'deleted them forever' from the **Bin**, so we can now show you how to upload newer files.

Fig. 4.21 Uploading Files.

Now, clicking the Upload button, gives you the possibility to upload both individual files and whole folders. However, the latter option is only available to you if you use Google Chrome as your Internet browser. Microsoft's Explorer can only upload files, so if you need the extra facility, you should install Google Chrome.

Clicking the Files link lets you browse your files on your computer to find the one you want to upload. Had you chosen to upload a folder, only folders will be displayed and you cannot open them to see what is inside them while browsing.

Below, we show the uploaded file, called **PC Users** and its preview (at the bottom right of the screen), which appears when you click the ⊙ link.

Fig. 4.22 Uploaded File and its Preview.

Clicking on the file name under TITLE, displays the file in the Google **Drive Viewer**, but you cannot edit it.

The types of files you can upload into Google **Drive**, are:

- For spreadsheets: .xls, .xlsx, .ods, .csv, .tsv, .txt, .tab
- For documents: .doc, .docx, .html, plain text (.txt), .rtf
- For presentations: .ppt, .pps, .pptx
- For drawings: .wmf
- For OCR: .jpg, .gif, .png, .pdf

A simpler way of uploading files to your **Drive** is by locating them on your computer and dragging them onto the screen of **My Drive**, as shown in Fig. 4.23 below.

Fig. 4.23 Dragging a File to Add on Google Drive.

Viewing and Editing Uploaded Files

To view such files on your devices you can either use the Google **Drive Viewer** or **Download** the file from Google **Drive**, by first selecting a file, then choosing one of the options from the drop-down menu of the **More** options at the top of **My Drive** screen, as shown in Fig. 4.24 on the next page.

When you open a Google document, spreadsheet, presentation or drawing, in **Drive Viewer**, it will launch in a new tab or window in your default browser.

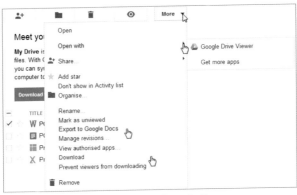

Fig. 4.24 The More Options.

A downloaded file from **My Drive** can only be edited if the program that created this file is installed on your device. A third option is to **Export to Google Docs** using the **More** drop-down menu options shown above.

An exported document to Google **Docs** can be edited from any of your devices. It does not require the program that created the original file. For example, the **Project 6** file shown below had an extra label added to it in cell A15 using a Tablet. The addition showed up on our PC instantly, as shown in Fig. 4.25 below.

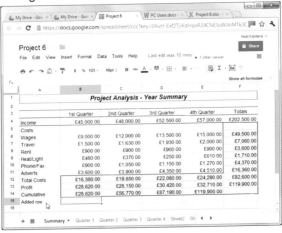

Fig. 4.25 Added Label on a Google Docs File.

Downloading Files from Google Drive

If you wanted to edit a file on Google **Drive** using the original program that created it, then you can download the file, by selecting the file and choosing the **Download** option from the right-click menu, as shown in Fig. 4.26.

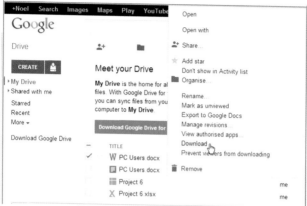

Fig. 4.26 The Right-click Menu for a Google Drive File.

The file is then opened (you'll be asked whether you want to save or open it) in the program that created it.

In Fig. 4.26 above, you can see the different pictorial representations of the two uploaded files and that of the exported files into Google **Docs**.

Creating Files on Google Drive

You can create a Google **Docs** file on Google **Drive** from any of your devices, by clicking the CREATE button. This opens a

drop-down menu of various types of files compatible with Google **Docs**, as shown here in Fig. 4.27. Clicking the **More** link near the bottom of the list, displays more options.

Fig. 4.27 Types of Files.

You can also create Google **Docs** from a list of **Templates** as shown in Fig. 4.28 below.

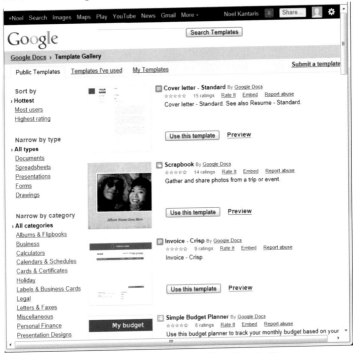

Fig. 4.28 Templates for Creating Google Docs.

Obviously there is a lot to choose from here. I suggest you spend some time exploring the various possibilities.

* * *

I leave it to you to explore Google **Drive** and Google **Docs** further, but always having in mind that Google **Docs** are files which you can access and edit on any of your devices, no matter where you are.

5

YouTube

You Tube   If you want to swap video clips with friends and familiy members, then **YouTube** is the right place for you. It is a video-sharing Web site, owned by Google, where anyone can view, upload and share video clips. According to Google Internal Data, people watch more than 2 billion video clips on **YouTube** every day, so it's really a huge repository of videos. **YouTube** is free as it is partially supported by advertising.

YouTube was first created in February 2005 but it caught on very quickly and only 18 months later Google purchased it for $1.65 billion. It has become so popular so quickly mainly because it is very easy to use. It accepts most common video formats and converts them so that they can be viewed over the Web without special software.

Anybody can upload video clips from their digital cameras or mobile phones, and friends can view them without worrying about the format. You can also e-mail the link to friends easily, or add **YouTube** generated code to your Web page or blog so a video can be played from that page.

Finding Your Way Around

To start **YouTube** you can type **www.youtube.com** into the **Address** bar of your browser and press the **Enter** key, or you can open it from the top of the Google **Navigation** bar by clicking the **YouTube** link, as shown in Fig. 5.1 below.

| +Noel | Search | Images | Maps | Play | YouTube | News | Gmail | Drive | Calendar | More - |

Fig. 5.1 The Google Navigation Bar.

Whichever method you use, a page similar to that in Fig. 5.2 should open. Please don't forget though that this site is changing all the time so it may not look quite the same.

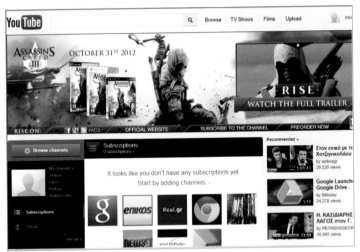

Fig. 5.2 A YouTube Opening Screen.

The Home Page

What strikes you first is a forthcoming film advert showing a short trailer and inviting you to watch the full trailer. Perhaps by the time you are reading this, Google might have changed their format and you might not see such an advert!

Once the short film trailer stops, several link tabs are displayed below it, as shown in Fig. 5.3 for the above trailer.

Fig. 5.3 The YouTube Link Tabs on the Home Page.

From here you can go to Facebook, Google + and Twitter, to the Official Website of the full film trailer, Subscribe to their Channel, or Pre-order the advertised film.

However, the very next day the above trailer changed to one that advertises a game with totally different type of links, so be warned that Google changes things daily!

The **YouTube** Home screen, shown in Fig. 5.2, has a **Search** box at the top. You enter text here to search for the type of video content you want to watch. This **Search** box has Google's search-suggest feature built-in, so you get query suggestions as you type like the ones in Fig. 5.4.

```
hist
history channel documentary
history channel
history
historia de un amor
history of the world part 1
history of rap
history of rap part 1
history is made at night smash
historia entre tus dedos
history of dance
```

Fig. 5.4 Search
Suggestions.

These suggestions are based on the most popular search queries sent in to Google. They should save a few keystrokes, reduce spelling errors, and "improve your search experience".

The **Home** page has several other sections: Next to the **Search** box there are several links, as shown in Fig. 5.5.

Fig. 5.5 Links to Videos, TV, Films or to the Upload Facility.

Clicking the Browse link, displays an array of today's 'Most Viewed Videos', part of which are shown in Fig. 5.6.

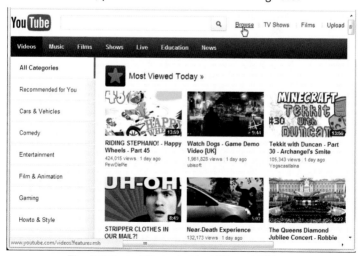

Fig. 5.6 Part of Today's Most Viewed Videos.

The next two links next to the **Search** box, after Browse, take you to Web pages full of TV Shows and Films with several categories each, as shown in Figs 5.7 and 5.8 below.

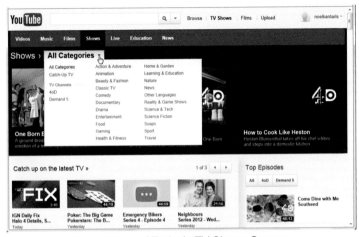

Fig. 5.7 Part of Today's TV Shows Screen.

Fig. 5.8 Part of Today's Films.

The Videos Page

Clicking the Videos link on a **YouTube** page, opens the videos page where you can more rapidly get a feel for **YouTube**. This has a list of video **Categories**, as shown in Fig. 5.9, and lets you quickly look through a list of the offered videos.

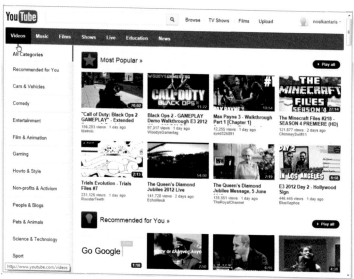

Fig. 5.9 Part of Today's Videos.

Apart from the various categories listed on the left of the page, you are also offered the **Most Popular** watched videos and, once you start using **YouTube**, you get an extra list under the **Recommended for You** section.

Each video listed has a title and image (you can click either to watch the video), a short description and some statistics, as shown in Fig. 5.10.

The Queen's Diamond Jubilee 2012 Live
141,728 views 2 days ago
Echoliteuk

Fig. 5.10 The Layout of a Typical YouTube Video Listing.

The Education Page

YouTube is so popular now that its users are not only individuals publishing short clips, but large corporate bodies, the Queen, universities and public departments. They consider **YouTube** to be a modern way to get their messages across. Many of the main Universities have hundreds of free lectures just waiting for you to view.

Fig. 5.11 below shows an example of some of the contents of the **EDU** page which was accessed by clicking the Education link. Note that under **All Categories** you have links for Primary & Secondary Education, University or Lifelong Learning.

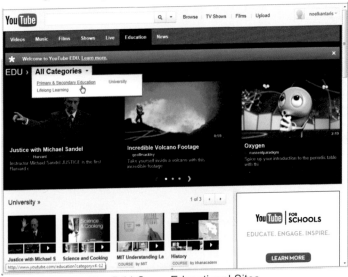

Fig. 5.11 Some Educational Sites.

Watching Videos

As we have seen, to watch a video you just click its thumbnail image or title link. Below the picture area is a toolbar which gives you some control.

Fig. 5.12 Video Playing Toolbar.

Clicking the video starts it. The first button on the toolbar in Fig. 5.12 is the **Pause** button , which when clicked changes to the **Play** button and restarts the video. With the **Slider**, you can move quickly through a video and see where you are. In our example above the slider reports just 36 second since the start of the video.

The other buttons on Fig. 5.12, have the following functions:

 Used to vary the sound level by dragging the slider.

Used to change the quality of the video, to HD mode.

Used to defer the time to when you prefer to watch the video.

 Used to expand the play area. When you click on it the **Shrink** button next to it is activated.

 Used to expand the play area to full screen. To return to the previous size, press the **ESC** key on the keyboard.

Below a playing video are five buttons shown in Fig. 5.13.

Fig. 5.13 Setting Playing Video Actions.

You can click the **Like** and **Dislike** buttons to vote on the video. The **Add to** button allows you to add the current video to **Favourites** or **Playlist** as shown in Fig. 5.14.

Add to playlist	☐ Add videos to top of list	Date created ▾
Favourites (1)	Public	
Enter new playlist name	Public ▾	Create playlist

Fig. 5.14 The Add to Button Options.

The **Share** button gives you several ways of sharing the video with your peers including the ability to **Embed** the video in your own Web page, or **E-mail** a link to someone. The last button can be used to **Flag** an inappropriate content.

To watch your **Favourites** or videos flagged as **Watch later**, just go to your 'Username' menu at the top of the page, click and choose appropriately (see also Fig. 5.17).

Uploading Videos to YouTube

Although unregistered users can watch most videos on the site, if you want to upload your own videos to **YouTube**, you must be registered and signed in to do so, just as you would have to be to use **Calendar**, **Gmail**, Google **+** and Google **Drive**. Please refer to Chapter 2 for details on how to do it.

The last link in the **Home** page of **YouTube** is the Upload, and clinking it displays the screen in Fig. 5.15 below.

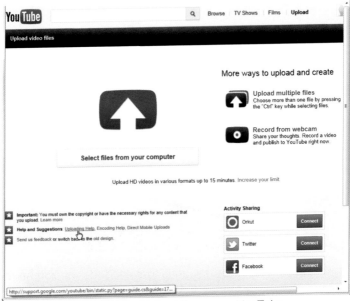

Fig. 5.15 The Upload Screen on YouTube.

It is remarkably easy to put your own video on **YouTube**, but make sure that your source video is of high resolution and that it conforms to a type supported by **YouTube**. For supported video formats and time limits, please click on the Uploading Help link pointed to in Fig. 5.15 on the previous page, as both the supported video types and time limits tend to be updated quite frequently.

Once you've finished making and editing your video, either click the Select files from your computer link or click the Upload multiple files link at the top right-hand corner of the page, or even create a video on your computer's webcam and upload it right now. However, to use this last option you must be very sure of your own abilities!

To illustrate the process we will assume you have created a video in advance, edited it and saved it on your computer. Clicking the Select files from your computer link, lets you browse to find your video and once selected it displays the screen in Fig. 5.16.

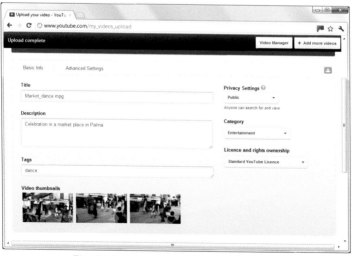

Fig. 5.16 Uploading a Video to YouTube.

A video takes only a few seconds to upload (depending on its length, of course), and once it is completed you should enter as much information about it as possible.

The type of information you need to supply includes a **Title**, some sort of **Description**, **Tags** and in what **Category** the video should be included. The more information you give, the easier it will be for users to find it! Choose whether you want your video set to **Public** or **Private**. If you make it private the only people that will be able to view it are those to whom you have given permission.

At the bottom of the screen in Fig. 5.16, you are given the option to select and use one of the displayed thumbnails to represent your video on the Web.

Managing your Own Videos

To see and manage your own videos, click on your 'Username' at the top of the **Home** page and on the displayed screen click the Video Manager link, as shown in Fig. 5.17.

Fig. 5.17 The Username Options Menu.

In our case, this opens the screen in Fig. 5.18, which shows all our uploaded videos.

Fig. 5.18 Managing your Own Videos.

To remove a video from your uploaded list, select it by clicking the small square to the left of it to check it, then click the Actions link and select **Delete** from the drop-down menu (Fig. 5.18).

There is a lot more to discover on YouTube, so go on and experiment!

6

Google Maps

 If you love maps this is the chapter for you. Google **Maps** help you to see a 2D view of the world both in map and satellite image format. You can use Google **Maps** to plan your holiday, search for locations and addresses, find local services, get driving or walking directions, or just to enjoy looking at its maps and satellite views. But if you are fond of a 3D view of the planet by joined satellite, aerial and street level photography, then have a look at Google **Earth** at the end of the book.

Google **Maps** functions are available all over the world and its satellite imagery covers the entire planet, but at varying levels of resolution. The map data for the UK is now provided by Europa Technologies and Tele Atlas.

The Google Maps Environment

Google **Maps** is an example of 'cloud computing' as you view maps in a Web browser and everything is downloaded from the Internet. The maps load quickly, especially if a reasonably fast broadband connection is available, otherwise a little patience might be needed!

Once your browser is open you can open Google **Maps** in one of several ways. You can type **maps.google.co.uk** into the **Address** bar of your browser and press the **Enter** key, you can click the **Maps** link in the Google **Navigation** bar of any Google UK page, as shown in Fig. 6.1, or you can type the location, or post code, followed by '**map**' into a Google Web **Search** box.

| +Noel | Search | Images | **Maps** | Play | YouTube | News | Gmail | Drive | Calendar | More ▾ |

Fig. 6.1 The Google Navigation Bar.

With the first two methods the opening screen should look like that in Fig. 6.2 below.

Fig. 6.2 The Opening Screen for the UK Google Maps.

If you get an opening map of the USA it means you started from a US Google page, not a UK one.

If you use the last method by providing a location, such as *clifton bristol* followed by '**map**', you get a screen similar to that in Fig. 6.3 below. Then, clicking the Clifton link, opens a screen similar to that of Fig. 6.2, but showing the specified location in Bristol in detailed view.

Fig. 6.3 A Search Screen for the UK Google Maps Using a Location.

Map Views

Fig. 6.4 The Earth &
Satellite Links in
Google Maps.

Depending on your location, there are different map views available in Google **Maps**. These are controlled by the two links at the top right map area, as shown in Fig. 6.2. When the mouse pointer hovers over these two links, it displays other links, as shown in Fig. 6.4 for Cornwall.

You click these links to change between the views. Clicking Earth changes the displayed links to Satellite and Map with different drop-down options. Clicking Map returns you to the screen of Fig. 6.4. In general, these links have the following effect:

Map – Displays a traditional style of map with a depiction of roads, borders, rivers, parks and lakes, etc.

Satellite – Displays satellite and aerial imagery of the same area. To show road and street names, click Labels on its drop-down options. The satellite images are not current and their quality depends on the locality.

Traffic – This link on the drop-down options in Fig. 6.4, provides visual traffic data for motorways and major trunk roads.

Terrain – This link on the drop-down options in Fig. 6.4, displays physical features on the map. Elevation is shown as shaded relief with contours when you are zoomed in. It also includes road numbers, street names and other information.

Earth – Changes the displayed links to Satellite and Map.

Perhaps it might be worthwhile spending some time here to see the effect of all these links – far too many to give precise description of their effect. Experimenting in this case is by far the best way of finding out for yourself.

Searching for a Location

If you want to find details of a particular location you just search for it. This is a Google program after all! You can search for an address, city, town, airport, county, country or continent by typing details in the **Search** box and clicking the **Search** button, as shown below.

Fig. 6.5 Entering a Search Address.

The result of this search is shown in Fig. 6.6 below. Google jumped to a map of the Cornish town, placed a Marker 📍 on it and showed the search result in text in the left pane of the page also with a marker.

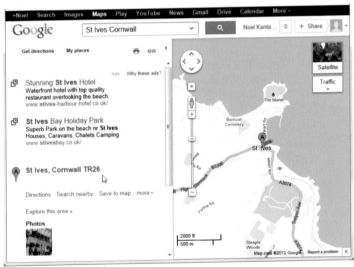

Fig. 6.6 The Result of a Search for a Town in Map View.

For specific addresses, entering them in the form of **Address, town, post code** usually gives the best results. You can also search for geographic features such as parks, mountains, lakes, etc., in the same way.

As shown in Fig. 6.6, the left pane can display photos, videos, and community maps based on the current map location. Clicking the **Explore this area** link displays arrays of photos, videos, and community maps that are found within the currently visible map boundary. A nice touch is that as you pan and zoom your map (see next page) everything updates dynamically, adding, removing and reordering the videos, pictures and maps available based on the new map area. Very slick.

To get more map viewing area, you can collapse the left panel by clicking the left arrowhead (◀) icon that appears just outside the top left corner of the map. Now clicking the displayed right arrowhead (▶) will reopen the pane. To get even more map room, maximise the window and go to your browser's **Full Screen** mode.

Searching for Services

No matter where you are in the country, you can use Google Maps to find the nearest business, educational or amusement service. Enter the appropriate words, followed by the words **in** or **near**, and the town, city or other location in the **Search** box. For example, typing *galleries in st ives cornwall* in the **Search** box, displays the screen in Fig. 6.7, provided you are using the UK Google maps.

Fig. 6.7 The Result of a Search for Galleries.

Google shows the results of the search in the left panel and a map of the area in the right panel with markers linked to the results.

Fig. 6.8 The Info Window.

If you click a marker, either alongside an entry in the left panel or on the map, an info window opens with details of that facility, as shown in Fig. 6.8.

Navigating the Map Area

With Google **Maps** you can change what shows in the map viewing area in two dimensions. You can pan the map (move it across the screen at the same scale), and you can zoom it in (to see a smaller area in more detail) or out (to see a larger area with less detail). You can navigate around a map using either the mouse or the supplied **Navigation** controls.

Using the mouse is much easier and quicker to do all the necessary operations. For example, to pan the map, just hold the left mouse button down to change the pointer to a hand ₍ᵐ₎ which you use to drag the map around the screen. To zoom, just roll the mouse wheel away from you to zoom in, and towards you to zoom out. The zoom will centre on the pointer location on the map. With these actions you can almost instantly zoom out to view the whole Earth, move the pointer to a new location and zoom in again to the scale you need. You can also centre and zoom in on a location, by double-clicking it on the map.

The **Navigation** controls shown here are placed in the top left corner of Google maps. To pan the map, you click the arrow buttons in the top grouping. Click ⌃ to move the map North, ⌄ to move it South, ❭ to move it East, or ❬ to move it West. Clicking the ₍ᵐ₎ icon in the centre will return you to your original view.

You can use the bottom grouping of the **Navigation** controls to zoom in + on the centre of the map, and − to zoom out. Dragging the zoom slider ⊝ up or down will zoom in or out. The 'Peg Man' icon 🚶 controls **Street View** (more on this later).

If you prefer using the keyboard, you can zoom in and out with the + and − keys. You can pan left ⇐, right ⇒, up ⇑, and down ⇓ with the arrow keys.

Getting Directions

There are several ways in Google **Maps** to get directions from one location to another.

Type a **from-to** statement into the search field, such as *from st ives to oxford*, and click the **Search** button.

Click the Get Directions link, enter a starting and ending location and click the **Get Directions** button.

Get directions from an info window (See Fig. 6.8).

Right-click on the map to get directions to that location.

The first method actually completes the operation as if you had used the second method, as shown in Fig. 6.9 below.

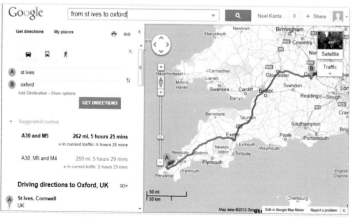

Fig. 6.9 Getting Driving Directions.

The program defaults to giving driving directions and the recommended route appears on the map as a blue line with

green markers at either end as shown in Fig. 6.9 on the previous page. Google **Maps** suggests suitable routes, breaks down its detailed directions (you have to scroll down to see these) into numbered sections in the left panel, and gives a total distance, as shown on the right in Fig. 6.10.

Fig. 6.10 The Suggested Route.

If you click on a route section in the left panel, an enlarged map opens. If the Peg Man icon appears you can click it to get **Street View** photos as well, as shown in Fig. 6.11. The Peg Man icon then turns blue so you can see what route section is active.

Fig. 6.11 Street View Information for a Section.

You can get new directions that **Avoid tolls** or **highways** (motorways in the UK) by clicking the **Show options** link in the **Get Directions** box. To reverse the directions for the return trip, click the ⇅ button. To change the starting or ending locations just retype them. To add a new location to the route, click the **Add destination** link to open another entry box, type in the location, and drag the box into the list wherever you want it. To change the distance units for directions, click **km** (kilometres) or **miles**. After making any changes make sure you click the **Get Directions** button.

When you study the proposed route on the map you may find you want to alter it. That's no problem with Google **Maps**. You can just click and drag a point on the blue directions line to any location on the map. Before you let go of the pointer a message flag shows the new distance and time for the trip taking that route. If you accept the new routing Google **Maps** immediately re-creates the directions on both the map and left panel. As an example, we decided to take the scenic route to Oxford, as shown in Fig. 6.12, but doing so has increased the journey time by 1 hour 15 minutes from the originally suggested route, even though it is less miles.

Fig. 6.12 The Scenic Route.

Public Transport

Depending on where you are, the **Public Transport** feature of Google **Maps** may let you map your trip using train, bus and coach transport. The system is not very complete, but you can update it on **www.google.com/transit**.

If transit information is available when you search for directions between start and end locations in Google **Maps**, the **By public transport** option will appear in the **Get Directions** box, as in Fig. 6.13 below.

Fig. 6.13 A Set of Public Transport Directions in Map View.

The times of departure of the various methods of public transport are given in the left panel. Again you'll have to scroll down to see these. To plan your trip in the future, click the down- arrowheads and select a new date and time.

This feature could be very useful, but until much better coverage is available in the UK you would be best using it with care.

Printing Google Maps

You can only print **Map View** maps and direction information in Google **Maps**, but not terrain maps or satellite imagery. With the map area you want to print on the screen you click the link at the top right of the window. A very clever interactive print preview page opens for you to customise what you print, including the option to **include large map**. If **Get Directions** was active in the left panel, it will print in the same format as Fig. 6.12 on the previous page.

If you click the Maps link on the print preview page, you will get small maps covering each section of the journey, as shown in Fig. 6.14 on the next page.

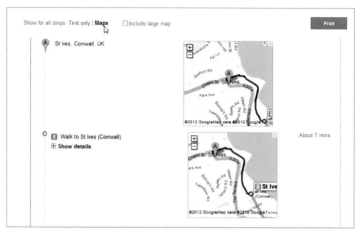

Fig. 6.14 Itinerary with Individual Section Maps.

If the **Street View** option appears in the top bar of the **Print Preview** window, you can select this to put interactive photos in your printed directions, as shown in Fig. 6.15 below.

Fig. 6.15 Street View Photos Included in a Print Preview.

Sharing Maps

If you click the **Link** ∞ button at the top of the Google Maps main window you can e-mail the current map or directions to a friend or colleague. This **Link** button when clicked displays the small window shown in Fig. 6.16.

Fig. 6.16 The Link Window.

From here you can either have a copy of the URL inserted in the body of an e-mail message when you click the **send** button, or copy and paste the HTML code to embed the current map into a Web page.

Traffic View

Google **Maps** has an exciting feature, that provides traffic data for the motorways and major A roads in England, Scotland, and parts of Europe, as shown in Fig. 6.17.

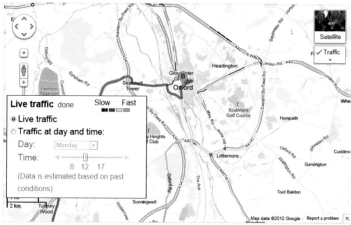

Fig. 6.17 Traffic View Around Oxford.

Whatever map view you are in, if you click the Traffic link, the parts of motorways and trunk roads that are subject to traffic hold ups will be overlayed with colour.

If your route shows red, it's stop-and-go for you, while green means it is probably clear. This is a very good feature when you are about to start your journey, but not so good if you are driving at the time, unless you have a tablet device with you!

When you are finished, click the Traffic link again to deselect it and turn off the feature.

Street View

Street View gives navigable 360° street-level imagery in Google **Maps**, and also in Google **Earth**. To obtain the imagery, Google sends specially adapted camera vehicles along the streets and roads to be covered, and these take full panoramic photos every few yards along the route. In Google **Maps** you can see images for each spot and take virtual walks or drives along that street. This lets you see what an area actually looks like, as if you were there in person.

You use the 'Peg Man' icon on the navigation controls to manipulate **Street View**. This only shows in orange if the feature is available anywhere in the open map area, otherwise it is greyed out. When you drag Peg Man off the Control Bar, roads covered by **Street View** appear with a blue border, as shown below for Oxford.

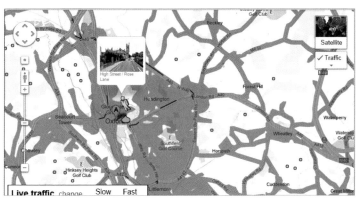

Fig. 6.18 Street View Coverage in Oxford.

Dragging Peg Man and dropping him on a street with a blue border will open **Street View** for that location, as shown in Fig. 6.19. A small location map is placed in the bottom-right corner, with Peg Man showing the current location. The green arrow shows the direction **Street View** is looking.

Fig. 6.19 Street View from the Bridge of Sighs in Oxford.

You can manipulate the view by dragging it right, left, up or down with your mouse, by using the arrow keys, or by clicking the ❯, ❮, ⌃ or ⌄ buttons on the navigation control. You can also drag the ⊟ on its outer ring as shown here.

To zoom in or out, click the + or – buttons, or double-click a point on the image to zoom in on it. If you are not zoomed in, the – button will move you out of **Street View** to the underlying map. In **Photo View**, large arrowheads appear at the bottom of the screen which you can use to zoom in and out.

As you move your mouse within **Street View**, you'll notice that the cursor has lightly-shaded 'shapes' attached to it – oval when your mouse is following a road, and rectangular when moving across the facades of buildings, called 'pancakes'.

Double-clicking on the pancake jumps you to the best panorama in that direction. Sometimes the pancake shows a little magnifying glass in the bottom right to indicate that double-clicking will zoom in on the current image rather than transport you to a closer location.

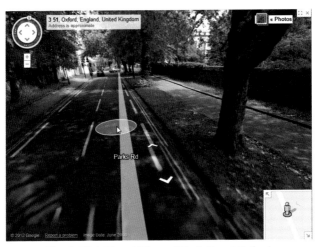

Fig. 6.20 A Street View of Park Road Oxford.

As shown in Fig. 6.20, the approximate street address is shown in the **Street View** window in a box that fades after a few seconds. Clicking on the arrows on the road propels you in the selected direction. Another feature that also fades is a box offering a selection of **Photos**. If you are in a popular location, clicking this should display a collection of photographs taken by other people from that location.

Once you have found the area you want to explore with **Street View**, we suggest you click the **Full screen** button to view a larger **Street View** area. To close **Street View** click the ⊠ button.

As you may have gathered, we use this feature a lot, especially when we are planning a vacation. If you ever find something inappropriate on Street View you should report it to Google. To do this, click **Report a problem** in the bottom-left of the image window, complete the form shown in Fig. 6.21 on the next page, and click **Submit**.

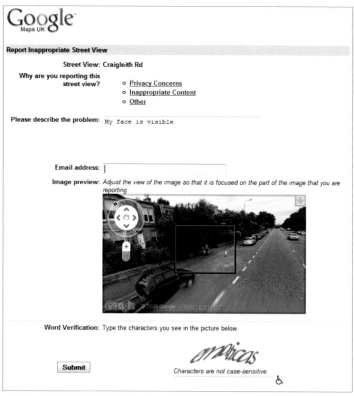

Fig. 6.21 Reporting an Inappropriate View to Google

Hopefully you will never have to do this, but we have seen some rather risqué photos before they have been removed!

7

Getting it Together

iGoogle

iGoogle is your personalised Google page. You can arrange for news, photos, weather and anything else that takes your fancy to be on your Google page and can even arrange for it to be your Home page so it is there in front of you when you open your Internet browser.

However, before we discuss how you can do it, let us show you how our iGoogle page displays.

Fig. 7.1 Our iGoogle Opening Page.

Normally we have Gmail expanded, but above it is shown minimised so that you can see as much of the page as possible. The other gadgets shown here are self-explanatory, that is, Maps, Weather and News.

The iGoogle Gadgets

iGoogle gadgets come in lots of different forms that make it easy to access the Web from your Home page. As you can see in Fig. 7.1 on the previous page, you can view your latest **Gmai**l messages, keep an eye on the weather and traffic and read the latest news headlines.

Some gadgets allow you to view its contents in full-page, called **Canvas** by Google. All you have to do is move your mouse pointer on the right part of the particular gadget's **Title** bar, to reveal the two links shown here. Click the one pointed to (top figure), to display the gadget in full screen. Click the link (bottom figure) to return the screen to its previous position.

Fig. 7.2 Options for Gadgets.

Clinking the down-arrowhead of the gear wheel on the left of each of the above links, displays a list of options, as shown in Fig. 7.2.

It is from here that you can select to **Minimize this gadget**, as we have done for Gmail in Fig. 7.1. You can then reverse the process by selecting the **Maximize this gadget** option.

There are three buttons at the top-right of the screen in

Fig. 7.3 Design Buttons.

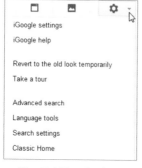

Fig. 7.4 The Options Menu.

Fig. 7.1, shown here in Fig. 7.3 with the labels that display when you hover the mouse pointer over each. You can use these buttons to design your **iGoogle** screen to your exact requirements. Clicking the down-arrowhead on the gear wheel button of Fig. 7.3, reveals a menu of options shown in Fig. 7.4. Do spend a bit of time examining the **iGoogle help** option.

Designing an iGoogle Home Page

Use either Google **Search** and type *igoogle uk* in the **Search** box, then click on the iGoogle – Google UK link, or go directly to

www.google.co.uk/ig

website. Whichever method you choose, the contents shown in Fig. 7.5 displays on your screen.

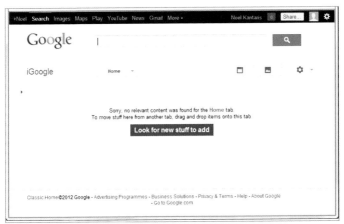

Fig. 7.5 The iGoogle Opening Page on your Browser.

Next, click the **Options** gear wheel at the top-right of the screen to open the options menu shown in Fig. 7.6 and select **iGoogle settings**, as shown here, which displays the **Settings** screen shown in Fig. 7.7 on the next page.

Fig. 7.6 Options Menu.

The first thing to do here is to change the **Language** to **English (UK)**, then type in the box provided the nearest **City** to your location or your postal code. You can change the tab name to something different from **Home**, if you wish, and finally select your page **Layout** (the default **2 columns** might be best).

Fig. 7.7 The iGoogle Settings Page.

Next, click the ⬚Save⬚ button to save the changes you have made so far. This action opens the screen in Fig. 7.8.

Fig. 7.8 The iGoogle Home Page.

You are now in a position to add your preferred gadgets by clicking the **Look for new stuff to add** link in Fig. 7.8. This opens a screen similar to that in Fig. 7.9 below.

Fig. 7.9 Selecting a Gadget for your iGoogle Page.

It is more than likely that by the time you look for new gadgets, Google would have changed not only the order in which they appear, but also the overall number available to you. Just scroll down to find what you want.

As you can see above, there are more than enough gadgets to satisfy anyone. Clicking the **Add it now** button, places the gadget on your iGoogle **Home** page and changes the button to **Added**, so you know. You just click one after the other for the gadgets that you want. Having added a gadget, you are also given the opportunity to look at other similar ones by clicking the You might also like ... link that appears below the **Added** button, but try not to be distracted too much!

The above procedure takes a lot longer to describe than it takes to carry out, so don't be put off. You might also like to have a look at the various options on the left of the screen.

When you finish examining more gadgets and the 'Editor's Choice', click the [Back to iGoogle] button to return to a screen similar to ours below. Finally, drag each gadget tile to the position the suits you best.

Fig. 7.10 The Designed iGoogle Home Page.

As you can see from the displayed map, some gadgets might require some fine tuning. For the map in Fig. 7.10 above, you will have to type in your default location so that your location displays rather that Google's headquarters! Watch out if you are tempted to select a theme, because having done so the only way to remove it is to go back to the screen of Fig. 7.7, click the Change theme link and change it back to **Classic**.

If you are the type who likes to be involved in **Chats**, then click the right-arrowhead to the left of **Weather** in Fig. 7.10 to open a **Chat** panel on the left of the screen. You can enable **Chat** and 'search for contacts' with whom to chat.

When you have enough chatting, you can close the **Chat** panel by clicking the left-arrowhead on its open panel which will also give more space for your gadgets to display in.

Making Your Design Your Home Page

To make your design your Home page, click the **Options** gear wheel, then choose in succession **iGoogle help**, **Learn about iGoogle**, **Personalize iGoogle**, then **iGoogle as my default homepage**. Choosing your browser from the displayed list shown in Fig. 7.11, produces specific instructions for that browser.

Fig. 7.11 Making iGoogle your Home Page.

If you find the above procedure too cumbersome and since, both **Internet Explorer** and **Google Chrome** are installed on our computer, we will show you an easier method to complete this task.

Making a Home Page in Internet Explorer

With your design opened in **Internet Explorer**, click the **Tools** gear wheel ⚙ and select **Internet Options** from the drop-down menu that displays. In the **General** tab of the displayed dialogue box, partially shown in Fig. 7.12 on the next page, click the **Use current** button, followed by the **Apply** and **OK** buttons at the bottom of the dialogue box.

Fig. 7.12 The Internet Options Dialogue Box.

Making a Home Page in Google Chrome

With your design opened in **Google Chrome**, click the **Customize** button and choose the **Settings** option in the displayed drop-down menu. In the **Settings** screen that opens, click to check the **Show Home button**, then the Change link and add **/ig** at the end of the displayed URL in the **Homepage** text box, followed by **OK**, as shown below.

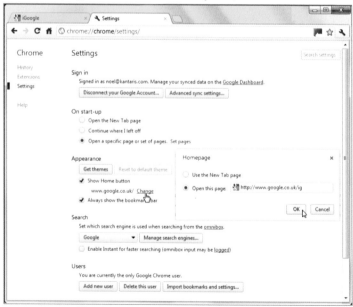

Fig. 7.13 The Homepage Dialogue Box.

8

Google Earth

 Google **Earth** gives an interactive globe on your computer. It streams Earth information, such as images, elevations, etc., to computers over the Internet. Using it, you can zoom and glide over satellite and aerial photos of the world, find nearby restaurants, measure the distance between two locations, do serious research, or go on virtual vacations. As a user you can explore the Earth and zoom down to cities, points of interest, buildings, bridges, roads and natural features, and it's fun.

Downloading Google Earth

The Google Earth program has to be downloaded from Google. To get it, go to **www.google.com/earth** which opens the screen shown in Fig. 8.1 below.

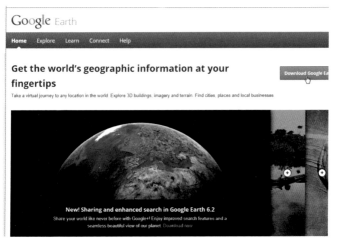

Fig. 8.1 Starting the Google Earth Download.

Clicking the Download link starts the procedure which took about 3 minutes for us. Make sure you remove the check marks from the two boxes that offer you to also download Chrome and make Chrome your browser's Home page, unless that is what you want. Having read the service agreement, click the **Agree and Download** button.

Google **Earth** opens with a view of the Earth from space, as shown in Fig. 8.2 below.

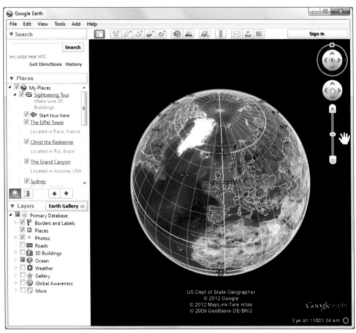

Fig. 8.2 The Google Earth Starting Window.

The globe appears in the right section of the program's window known as the **3D viewer** which is always open. On the left side of the window is a sidebar with three panels. The **Search** panel is used to find places and directions and manage search results. The **Places** panel is used to locate, save and organise placemarks, and the **Layers** panel lets you 'switch on and off' available layers which display specific features in the **3D viewer**.

To get more room for the **3D viewer**, you can close the sidebar by clicking the **Hide Sidebar** button ⬚ on the toolbar of the Google **Earth** menu bar. To show the sidebar when it is closed just click the button again.

Navigating the Globe

Dragging the left mouse button ☝ on the globe will gently rotate it in the direction you drag. On a flat map this is the panning action. Double-clicking the mouse buttons, rotating the middle scroll wheel of the mouse, or dragging the right mouse button, will zoom you in or out. If you drag the mouse with the middle scroll wheel depressed you can tilt the globe. We find these are the easiest ways to 'get around' the Earth, and suggest you practise them on the whole globe, as it is easier to see the results.

Navigation Controls

If you move the pointer over the upper right-hand corner of the **3D viewer**, the **Navigation Controls** appear, as shown in Fig. 8.2. If they don't, use the **View**, **Show Navigation** menu commands and select **Automatically**. You can turn them off again this way later if you don't like them. These controls offer the same navigation action as the mouse but you can also swoop and rotate your view.

The **Look** joystick at the top lets you look around from a single vantage point. Click an arrow to look in that direction or press down on the arrow to change your view. Dragging the outer ring rotates the view. Clicking the **North-up** button resets it with North at the top.

The **Move** joystick, in the middle, moves your position from one place to another. Click an arrow to look in that direction or press down on the mouse button to change your view. After clicking an arrow, move the mouse around on the joystick to change the direction of motion.

Dragging the **Zoom** slider ⊖ up or down will zoom in or out incrementally, or click **+** to zoom in on the centre of the **3D viewer**, and **−** to zoom out. As you move closer to the ground, Google **Earth** tilts to change your viewing angle to be parallel to the Earth's surface. You have to play with all these to get used to their actions.

Some Sightseeing

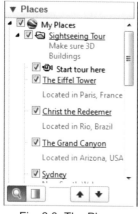

Fig. 8.3 The Places Panel.

Fig. 8.3 displays the **Places** panel with the **Sightseeing Tour** folder in the panel shown open in the displayed screen. Double-clicking an entry will zoom Google **Earth** to that location. Try it.

If you select the folder itself and double-click the 🗺 **Start tour here** entry, it will work its way through the list, zooming in to each location. To spend more time at a location just press the **Pause** ‖ button, and to continue press the **Play** ▶ button, shown below.

My Places

The **Places** panel contains two main folders, **My Places** and **Temporary Places**, but you have to scroll down to see the latter. You can use the **My Places** folder to save and organise places that you visit, searches and natural features.

Setting Placemarks

Maybe the first location most people would want to 'placemark' is their home. To do this, first find the position you want in the **3D viewer**, preferably by searching, then choose the best viewing level for the location and click the **Placemark** 📌 button on the toolbar at the top of the window.

The **New Placemark** box opens and a **New Placemark** icon is placed in the **3D viewer** inside a flashing yellow square. Drag this **Placemark** to the location you want, as shown in Fig. 8.4, and fill in the open box. You should give the **Placemark** a name, perhaps add a description and set the style, colour and opacity of the marker. Clicking the **OK** button sets your **Placemark** in the **3D viewer** and as a new entry in the **My Places** folder, as shown in Fig. 8.5.

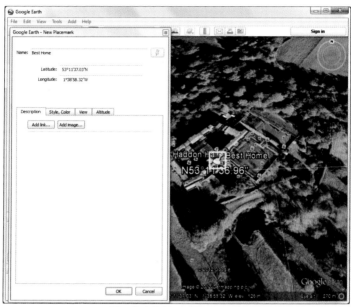

Fig. 8.4 A New Placemark.

In the future when you want to go to this location no matter

where you are, just double-click its entry in the **My Places** folder.

Fig. 8.5 The New Location in Places.

Searching for Places

You can use the **Search** box at the top-left corner of the screen to type the name of a famous place, restaurant, or other service and watch Google **Earth** fly to it. For example, typing *Edinburgh Castle* and clicking the Search button, displays the fantastic aerial scene shown in Fig. 8.6.

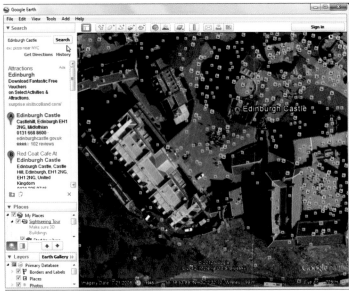

Fig. 8.6 Aerial View of Edinburgh Castle.

As you can see, there are hundreds of photos that you can click to enlarge and enjoy.

The two buttons below the **Search** box, **Get Directions** and **History**, give you more information worth investigating.

Getting Directions

To get directions in Google **Earth** is very similar to the procedure in Google **Maps**. The main way is to enter start and ending locations in the two boxes that display when you click the **Get Directions** and click the Get Directions button.

Once you have a route displayed in the **3D viewer**, you can use the **View in Google Maps** ▣ button on the toolbar at the top of the screen to give you the information in a more manageable format. You can also **Print** such information, or send it to someone by **E-mail**, using the two buttons adjacent to the **View in Google Maps** on the toolbar.

Street Views in Google Earth

Fig. 8.7 shows a street view of the M6 Motorway while on our way to the North.

Fig. 8.7 Street View of the M6 Motorway.

As you can see, this is similar to the **Street Maps** discussed in Chapter 6, therefore it might be a good idea if you refer to that section of Chapter 6 for guidance on how to manipulate a **Street View**.

Layers

Google Earth can provide a lot of information about a location, and viewing all such information at once, can be very confusing. To get over this, it stores its information in layers, which you can turn on or off. Layers include data for such things as ocean, weather, photos, roads, borders, labels, restaurant guides, street names and 3D buildings.

Layers are created by Google or its partners and are stored in the **Layers** panel area on the lower left-hand side of Google **Earth**'s screen, shown here in Fig. 8.8. You turn on a layer by clicking the check-box next to its name and turn it off by removing the tick in the check box.

Try exploring the content of the **Layers** panel by opening up all the folders and trying each option in turn. The **Gallery** folder contains some amazing, very high resolution photography and lots of other surprising things. In the **More** folder you can get Google **Earth** to show you specific types of places, such as hospitals, churches, petrol stations, etc., the list is very long and more are being added all the time.

Fig. 8.8 The Layers Panel.

Historical Imagery

As you move over the globe the aerial photography date is shown in the bottom-left corner of the **Earth** window. If a clock  icon appears here it means **Historical Imagery** is also available for you to view. Clicking the year alongside it will open a slider which you can use to change the viewing date.

Extra Terrestrial Google

The latest versions of Google **Earth** let you explore the sky at night, as well as the Moon and Mars. You access all of these in the **3D viewer**, with options obtained when you use the **Switch between Earth, Sky and other planets** button, as shown in Fig. 8.9 on the next page.

Google Sky

This lets you see a view of the night sky and explore the stars, constellations, galaxies and planets from your computer. Thanks to partners such as the Hubble Space Telescope, you can see some superb imagery of space.

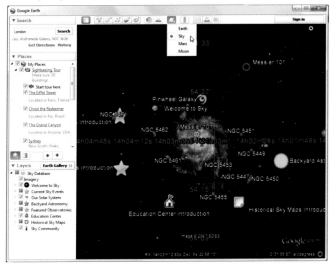

Fig. 8.9 Google Sky.

Below we show two camera shots of Mars and the Moon.

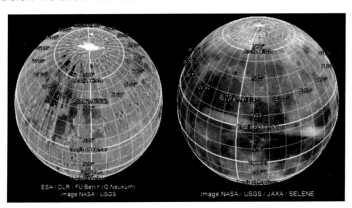

Fig. 8.10 Google Mars (Left) and Google Moon (Right).

If you find these extra terrestrial features of Google **Earth** of interest, use your browser and go to **www.google.com/sky**.

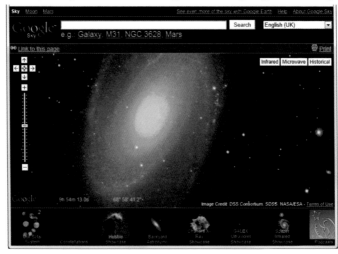

Fig. 8.11 Galaxies at Google.com/sky.

Image Quality

Google gets the images presented on Google **Earth** from satellite and aerial photos, which they then 'stitch together' to make what you see. Sometimes the images themselves are of varying quality. Larger cities are usually sharp and in focus, but more remote areas can be pretty poor.

The image stitching technique sometimes leaves problems with accuracy. Road overlays and labels often look like they are a little out of place. So it is not surgically precise, but it's free after all!

Overall we think Google **Earth** is a lot of fun. It's fantastic as an educational tool to let children (both young and old) explore the World. Google **Maps** and Google **Earth** make planning road trips and vacations much easier. If you like looking at and using maps and enjoy your computer, then it is worth your while spending some time mastering these Google applications. Good luck and have fun!

Index